in GOD'S TIME

in GOD'S TIME

TRUE STORIES OF TRANSFORMATION AND ANSWERED PRAYER

EDITORS OF GUIDEPOSTS

A Gift from Guideposts

Thank you for your purchase! We want to express our gratitude for your support with a special gift just for you.

Dive into *Spirit Lifters*, a complimentary e-book that will fortify your faith, offering solace during challenging moments. Its 31 carefully selected scripture verses will soothe and uplift your soul.

Please use the QR code or go to **guideposts.org/ spiritlifters** to download.

In God's Time

Published by Guideposts
100 Reserve Road, Suite E200
Danbury, CT 06810
Guideposts.org

This book was compiled with the assistance of James Stuart Bell.

Cover and interior design by Serena Fox, Bean Inc.
Cover photo © Shutterstock
Typeset by Aptara, Inc.

ISBN 978-1-961441-05-7 (softcover)
ISBN 978-1-961441-06-4 (epub)

Printed and bound in the United States of America
10 9 8 7 6 5 4 3 2 1

ECCLESIASTES, CHAPTER 3
in the
KING JAMES VERSION:

1. To every thing there is a season, and a time to every purpose under the heaven:

2. A time to be born, and a time to die; a time to plant, and a time to pluck up that which is planted;

3. A time to kill, and a time to heal; a time to break down, and a time to build up;

4. A time to weep, and a time to laugh; a time to mourn, and a time to dance;

5. A time to cast away stones, and a time to gather stones together; a time to embrace, and a time to refrain from embracing;

6. A time to get, and a time to lose; a time to keep, and a time to cast away;

7. A time to rend, and a time to sew; a time to keep silence, and a time to speak;

8. A time to love, and a time to hate; a time of war, and a time of peace.

TABLE OF CONTENTS

INTRODUCTION

"To every thing there is a season . . ."
—Ecclesiastes 3:1 (KJV)

These words usher in some of the most well-known and well-loved verses in the Bible, the opening of chapter 3 in the book of Ecclesiastes—a contemplation of the way that times come and go throughout our lives, and a reminder of how God guides us through all our seasons.

When we asked writers to share how those verses have applied to their own experience, we were moved by the stories we received. They wrote about pivotal moments and small victories, losses mourned but also laughter and joy, and being lifted out of hard times by God's ever-present guiding hand. We're excited to bring those stories to you.

Each chapter in this volume centers around one of the verses from Ecclesiastes 3:2 to 3:8. In chapter 1 ("a time to be born, and a time to die; a time to plant, and a time to pluck up that which is planted"), we have stories of births and passings alongside times of planting seeds for a brighter future—and harvesting seeds planted long ago.

Chapter 2 ("a time to kill, and a time to heal; a time to break down, and a time to build up") considers what happens when you "kill" a bad habit or the negative emotions that have been keeping you bound and then embrace the healing that results.

Chapter 3 ("a time to weep, and a time to laugh; a time to mourn, and a time to dance") shows us the necessity of taking time to mourn, the power of laughter to bring us through hard times, and the joy of dancing.

Chapter 4 ("a time to cast away stones, and a time to gather stones together; a time to embrace, and a time to refrain from embracing") brings us unexpected gifts at just the right time and stories that show us the rewards of knowing when to embrace—be it other people or the circumstances in our lives—and when to refrain.

Chapter 5 ("a time to get, and a time to lose; a time to keep, and a time to cast away") continues that theme as our writers tell stories of loss and gain on both a large and small scale and the serenity that came from letting go of the material things that they no longer needed.

Chapter 6 ("a time to rend, and a time to sew; a time to keep silence, and a time to speak") brings us sewing in both a literal and a metaphorical sense, paired with hard-earned lessons on knowing when to bite your tongue and when to let the words flow.

In Chapter 7 ("a time to love, and a time to hate; a time of war, and a time of peace"), we wrap up with some beautiful love stories, followed by stories of war—both with others and with themselves—that resolved into a true sense of peace.

Each chapter is expertly introduced by longtime Guideposts contributor Shirley Raye Redmond, who draws on her love of history to tell the stories of people who embodied these verses in their own lives, in the process setting an example for generations to come. In addition to the introductions, each chapter contains a "time to reflect" on how these themes can apply to our own lives, and a closing prayer to tie everything together.

We hope that you'll be uplifted by the stories contained in this book and inspired to look at these verses in a whole new way.

—Editors of Guideposts

CHAPTER
1

BEGINNINGS AND ENDINGS

ECCLESIASTES 3:2

A time to be born,
and a time to die;
a time to plant,
and a time to pluck up that which is planted

INTRODUCTION

Stories of birth, death, planting, harvesting, and profound transformations in between

— By Shirley Raye Redmond —

BRAVE. LOVING. WISE. Persistent. Missionary Elisabeth Elliot (1926–2015) was all these things and more, demonstrating courage and forgiveness in the midst of mourning and the patience to plant a love of Jesus in others that would take years to bear fruit.

While growing up in a devout Christian family in Germantown, Pennsylvania, Elisabeth—known to everyone around her as Betty— met several visiting missionaries. She sat enraptured at her family's dining-room table, listening to their life-and-death accounts of sharing the gospel in faraway lands.

After attending Wheaton College in Illinois, where she studied classical Greek, Betty longed to translate the New Testament for an unreached group of people. Following her marriage to Jim Elliot in 1953, the pair joined four other families on the mission field in Ecuador. There Betty gave birth to their only child—a baby girl they named Valerie. It was a time of great joy. The dedicated young couple felt a strong sense of purpose as they sowed the seeds of God's truth among the peaceful Quechua tribe. Betty kept a detailed journal of their experiences.

But then the dream became a nightmare. Jim and four other missionaries were murdered while making overtures to the nearby Waorani people, who had a history of suspicion of outsiders and violence against any strangers entering their territory. Images of the aftermath of the attack taken by a photojournalist for *Life* magazine, who accompanied the American rescue team, caused a sensation around the world. Faithful in the midst of her grief, Betty insisted, "This is not a tragedy. God has a plan and purpose in all this."

And He did. Shortly after the death of the five men, Betty and the sister of one of the murdered missionaries, Rachel Saint, were allowed to live among the Waorani.

Betty believed that by freely forgiving those who'd killed her husband, she might be able to demonstrate God's mercy and grace. With her toddler on her hip, Betty and Rachel moved into a tiny, rain-swept hut. They ate roasted monkey meat and other local fare while painstakingly translating the story of Jesus into a language the Waorani could understand.

Her courageous faith won many in the tribe to Jesus. Her book about her experiences, *Through the Gates of Splendor*, sold more than half a million copies when it was first released and inspired millions of readers around the world.

Betty married again and wrote several more inspirational bestsellers. She also began a speaking ministry across the United States, becoming one of the most influential Christian women of our time. When she died at the age of 89, Betty left behind a legacy of faith and a reminder to us all: "God never denies our heart's desire except to give us something better."

IN ELISABETH ELLIOT we have someone who embodied not only endurance in the face of her husband's death, but the courage to plant the seeds of peace in the hearts of people who had embraced death and violence. Throughout this chapter you'll find more stories that speak to the themes of Ecclesiastes 3:2, stories of births and deaths, of dreams delayed and later fulfilled, and of the joys of reaping a harvest sown in hope.

A SLOW BABY BOOM

— By Caroline S. Cooper —

"IT'S A BABY! It's a baby!"

The voice—my voice—sounded muffled and slurred. I twisted on the bed, eyes closed, trying to remember what had happened. A baby had cried; a joyful sound. My husband, Harry, and I were excited about starting our family—so, why did my heart ache?

I overheard a conversation as the anesthesia began to subside.

A young voice quivered, "Mrs. Cooper started rolling around and pulled out her IV."

A knowing voice responded. "She had a procedure to determine if she could have children, and the baby's cries must have disturbed her."

Memories flooded back as I opened my eyes in the hospital recovery room. I thought about the first long year we'd endured without the hoped-for pregnancy, followed by another year of using fertility medication with no effect. We had recruited prayers from family, friends, and our Sunday school class. We trusted God heard us yet continued to wait for His response.

After that second year, Harry and I held hands in my obstetrician's office as Dr. Larry Batty advised me to undergo an outpatient procedure, a hysterosalpingography (HSG), to visually examine my womb. He would use the results to determine our next steps. Harry and I looked at each other. We had no other options at the moment. We would go through this together.

My dad had accompanied me to the hospital on the day of the procedure, and I heard his concerned voice as he entered the room.

"Why's she so pale? What are you doing to help her?"

I could only imagine his pain at seeing his child in a situation he could not control. But I was so thankful he had come with me. I tried to push aside the internal voice that reminded me that Harry had gone to work instead of joining me at the hospital. I knew he handled his fear by avoiding the situation, but didn't he realize how much I needed him?

"Your daughter will be fine," the nurse told Dad confidently.

When Dr. Batty entered the room, my heart began to beat faster.

"Everything looks fine with your anatomy," Dr. Batty said with a kind smile. "I see no physical reason why you should not get pregnant. Unfortunately, this means there must be another issue. Let's take a break from treatment, and I'll recommend a fertility specialist in the fall."

I nodded, unable to speak. Even though I half expected this result, the reality hit hard. No more fertility medicine. No more monthly blood work. No more pregnancy tests. I did not look forward to the long summer.

Dad drove me home and tucked me into my recliner. I could not bring myself to call Harry. He had abandoned me. He would have to wait until he came home to hear the news. I sank into my pain and anger, which was directed not only at my husband but also at God. We served Him faithfully. Why didn't He answer?

I woke from a fitful nap to see Harry had returned.

"Sweetheart, how did it go?" he asked.

When I told him the news, we cried. Then we prayed: "God, where are You? Why aren't You answering us? Please give us a child. We want to start our family."

Our surging emotions almost tore us apart. I felt alone and confused. He felt helpless and concerned. Over the months that followed, we learned a lot about the importance of communication and understanding in building a solid marriage, although it took a while for me to accept his apologies and truly forgive him for "abandoning" me. God gave us that time to strengthen our bond as husband and wife before we welcomed a child. We had to acknowledge God as the master creator and wait for His plan to unfold.

A couple of months after our last doctor's visit, I noticed a strange soreness. At first, I thought I had overexerted myself in our weekly church softball game. Then came a hint of nausea and fatigue. I ran the signs of pregnancy through my mind. To our delight, the in-office pregnancy test confirmed the home test.

"It looks like you're going to be parents." Dr. Batty said. "I have to tell you, though, this should not have happened. Your last blood work showed no possibility of pregnancy."

I could see his scientific mind mulling over this turn of events. Joyfully I exclaimed, "This is a miracle. God did this!"

God's miracle, in His perfect time. We had been so focused on *our* desire to have a child in *our* timing that we missed seeing *God's* blessings while we waited. Our commitment to each other had matured. We recognized that God modeled a perfect parent by teaching us patience and how to trust in Him. We were humbled by God's generosity in trusting us to nurture a child.

"IT'S A BABY! It's a baby!"

My words were filled with awe as the nurse placed our baby in my arms. Harry gently caressed Jimmy's face. The anguish of the past 2 years was replaced by joy and praise.

When Jimmy turned one, God moved in our hearts to have another child. Dr. Batty recommended fertility medicine again. We agreed. Even though we had witnessed God's miraculous intervention with my first pregnancy, we wanted all the help we could get.

How often do we witness the power of God only to have doubts He will come through again?

I became pregnant 1 month later, before the medication had a chance to work. God had again blessed us in His time by swiftly answering our prayers. Susan came into the world 22 months after her brother.

About this time, our insurance changed networks. With a heavy heart, we said goodbye to Dr. Batty. He had witnessed our first two miracle babies. My new doctor saw nothing unusual when I became pregnant, but I know Dr. Batty would have marveled again when the pregnancy occurred without medication or other procedures, only God's power and grace. Jimmy and Susan could not wait to hold their baby sister, Rebekah.

> He settles the childless woman in her home as a happy mother of children. Praise the Lord.
> —Psalm 113:9 (NIV)

Three months later, I began experiencing deep depression. I failed in my attempts to push through tears and exhaustion. My family needed a healthy mom. After multiple doctor visits, l learned that my experience had a name: postpartum depression. In time it passed, but it left a lasting impact on our family.

Even though we had wanted four children, Harry and I felt we could not risk putting our kids through agony if Mom's postpartum depression returned. There would be no more babies. I felt defeated, even while praising God for giving us three wonderful children.

A year or so later, my garage sale had all the signs of success as people milled around the no-longer-needed baby items.

"How much for the high chair?"

"I'll give you five bucks for this booster seat."

"These clothes are so cute!"

Baby items were always in demand. But watching people handle my precious possessions filled me with sadness and longing. I pulled the items back into the garage.

God whispered, "Your family is missing someone."

When I told Harry my feelings, he admitted that he, too, had thought of another child. Thanks to another insurance change, we returned to Dr. Batty. This time, he showed no surprise when I became pregnant.

When the nurse placed our fourth miracle baby in my arms, I could barely breathe; I realized this precious bundle would not be here if Harry and I had not responded to God's nudging. As an added blessing, I did not have postpartum depression.

Harry and I have no doubt that God planned our family. In His way. In His perfect time. We wept, prayed, and grew closer through the experience. We recognized children as a gift and blessing from our amazing God. We learned to trust that God will never leave us or forsake us, no matter what we experience in life. And we learned that God's plan is much better than ours.

A time to be
born, and a
time to die

OUR LIGHT IN A DARK HOUR

— By Christina Rich —

"HAPPY NEW YEAR!" Luke, my adult son, said. He muttered something under his breath after that, and then quickly shut our door.

I glanced at my husband. I couldn't tell by James's expression if he knew what he heard or only suspected. We were both tired and exhausted. It was after one in the morning and the fact that James was up past ten was an odd occurrence, especially since he hadn't stayed up to ring in the new year for many years.

"What did he say?" James asked, his brow furrowing deeper by the second as his confusion cleared. It was obvious he didn't like what he thought he heard. I, on the other hand, was thrilled.

"He said Emma is pregnant."

"That's what I thought he said." James's cheeks burned bright with anger. "I want more for him. He's my son! I don't want him having kids young."

I leaned against the wall and listened as he listed off all the reasons why our 20-year-old son and his 18-year-old girlfriend shouldn't be having a child. A wave of emotions rolled through me and over me. I understood his points, and yet I wanted to be happy. After all, I was going to be a grandma, and life, no matter the circumstances, is precious. We needed life. The last year had been challenging in terms of funerals. Five had been too many. Before our son made his surprise announcement, I'd even mentioned something to the effect that we'd attended more funerals than weddings recently. It was time for a happy event, and what better time for God to allow it to happen?

"Don't you have anything to say?"

I nodded. "Do we believe God's Word?"

"Yes." He narrowed his eyes a little. We'd just spent all of New Year's Eve at the rescue mission in a role of ministering to the homeless, to the hopeless. I could tell he already didn't like what I was going to say.

"Well, if we're going to believe in it, we need to believe in its entirety. Psalm 139 says, 'You created my inmost being; you knit me together in my mother's womb.' That is all I need to know to accept this and be happy."

Another word was not spoken between us on the issue. I do not know what he thought after that. I don't know if he accepted the fact that we would become grandparents with joy or with disappointed resignation. Outside the announcement that we would have a grandson come June, we didn't speak much about the coming baby, not until the day of his birth, which would come during one of the greatest trials our family would experience.

"I HAVE AN ulcer," James told the physician's assistant. He'd spent that last week or so with stomach cramps. Today, he'd given in and asked me to take him to an urgent care facility. I did. They weighed him, and we both laughed when they told us he was nearly 160 pounds.

"Gosh, you've lost a lot in the last few weeks," I said. But he'd quit smoking a year before, and suddenly his never-changing weight had ballooned. We'd been joking that we both needed to lose weight.

"I don't think this is an ulcer, Mr. Smith." The physician's assistant looked grim. "You need to go to the emergency room."

Air refused to flow easily to and from my lungs. What wasn't she telling us?

"I just need some antibiotics—"

"No, Mr. Smith, you need to see someone more qualified than myself."

Six hours later, after seeing the on-call doctor and listening to James tell the doctor he had an ulcer, we left the ER without the scans the doctor wanted to perform and the prescription for antibiotics James insisted on having. The last words the doctor said to us beat against my chest like a battering ram. "Whatever this is, it will still be here in a few weeks. I'll see you then."

He'd see us then? Thinking back on this moment, I wondered why the doctor hadn't burst James's tenacious belief he had an ulcer and just told us the truth of what he suspected.

A FEW WEEKS later, at the end of May, Emma had grown big with our first grandchild, and James had dwindled to nothing more than skin and bones. A few days after the antibiotics ran their course, James and I argued. I had tried multiple times to get him back to the ER, but he wouldn't go. He finally screamed at me, saying he didn't have cancer. The room stilled for a small moment. The thought had never even crossed my mind. I stared back at him and in a panicked voice told him he was forcing his children to watch him starve to death and it wasn't fair. Yeah, I played the kid card. You had to have known James. He was stubborn, beyond stubborn, and he rarely believed anything I had to say. If it concerned his kids, that was a different matter. The next day, my father and I loaded James into the car, and we drove him back to the ER.

The diagnosis was frightening. James didn't just have cancer. He had cancer in every organ and most of his bones. The doctors offered hope. They offered treatment. They told us if he started radiation, he'd have longer to live. James didn't want it. He didn't want any treatment at all. We stayed in a sterile room for a week before we returned home. However, before he left, he finally agreed to the radiation.

Your eyes saw my unformed body; all the days ordained for me were written in your book before one of them came to be.
—Psalm 139:16 (NIV)

That first treatment was scheduled for a few days after we took him home. It was the only one he would ever have.

Right in the middle of this fight for his life, Emma went into labor. I left James's side for a few hours to go to the hospital, but this time, instead of pacing in hopelessness wondering how we'd win the fight against such an aggressive cancer, I was pacing anxiously with hope, waiting to hold that new little life in my hands. The labor was long, and Emma wanted only Luke and her best friend in the room. I was okay with that. I remembered wanting to preserve my dignity in front of a bunch of strangers. I would wait. Just as it was time for me to go back home to see to James's needs—he couldn't walk or use the restroom, and he needed full bedside assistance—an entire team rushed into the delivery room. I knew that didn't mean anything good, so I waited until I heard that Emma and the baby were okay.

I found out later there had been an issue with the delivery. I don't know how close we came to losing mother and son, but it was close.

The little guy came home with us, and each time James's care became overwhelming, I would slip out of our bedroom and seek out the newborn. I would hold him, sing to him, and gaze into his little gray eyes filled with so much life. I noticed my daughters and son doing the same.

James took a turn for the worse on Father's Day, less than a month after his diagnosis and 2 weeks after our grandson was born. I had been caring for him, trying to give him sips of water. His tongue cleaved to the roof of his mouth. I called the on-call cancer doctor, and he told me it was impossible for James to have progressed that quickly and to bring him in on Monday. I didn't. Noticing the purpling on the skin of his legs and other extremities, I knew his body was shutting down. I called 911. He stayed overnight in the hospital, barely conscious, barely breathing. The next day, we transported him to hospice. Twelve hours later, he was gone.

In the days following his death, my grandbaby kept me afloat. I would rock him and sing to him, focusing on the promise for the future. Having the little guy in our lives helped me and our children through stunned grief.

The birth of my grandchild and the death of my husband within weeks of each other could only have been God's perfect timing. James's days were ordained by God, and God knew when James would take his last breaths, just as He knew when our first grandbaby would take his first breaths. Somehow, God was gracious enough to send that baby to bring a whole lot of light to our family in the midst of a dark hour. He was a balm to our grieving hearts.

A time to be
born, and a
time to die

FIVE HUNDRED CHURCHES IN GOD'S TIME

— As told to Sandy Kay Slawson —

EVANGELIST JAY MATTHEWS parked his 1958 Oldsmobile in front of the First Assembly of God Church in Pascagoula, Mississippi. After a short prayer with his traveling companion, Oscar, he rolled up his window and stepped out. Sweat dampened his button-down shirt. The harsh Mississippi heat didn't negate God's call. He straightened his tie and waved to the pastor under the portico.

"Pastor Medlock, meet Oscar Jones from Mercedes, Texas. He'll be my translator in Mexico."

"Good to meet you, Mr. Jones." Pastor Medlock shook Oscar's hand. "Did the Georgia revival go well?"

"It changed from a 1-week tent meeting to 3. Many souls were saved," Jay said.

"Hallelujah, winning souls for Christ."

"I was born of the Spirit at a revival in '49 myself," Jay said.

"Twenty years later, your mission field still expands, and you've set a fine example, Jay."

"Ecclesiastes 3 says there's a time for everything. To be there when it's time for a new Christian to be born is my favorite thing," Jay said.

"Mine, too, brother. Well, we've got supper and beds for y'all and clothes for the orphanages."

"Just the food and gifts, please. We want to travel a few more hours today." Jay glanced toward Oscar, who nodded.

"OSCAR, THEY LOADED this car till the bumper is about to hit the highway."

"We'll switch to my station wagon in Mercedes."

Once across the border near Progreso, Texas, they bumped along the rutted roads. An hour into Mexico, a pop alerted Jay to their flat tire. He eased off the road and woke Oscar.

"I'll get the tools," Oscar said.

Jay removed the hubcap and lug nuts before Oscar brought the spare. Oscar put the jack underneath the car's frame and pumped. Jay pulled the flat free. Oscar rolled it away.

"Agh!" Jay dropped the spare. A tarantula crawled back inside the tire rim.

"What?"

"There's a tarantula in the spare."

"It probably came from Mercedes. I'll get rid of it." Oscar grabbed the lug wrench, and hit the spare until the tarantula appeared, then hit the beast like a baseball and sent it flying into the brush. "There, it's gone."

Jay shuddered.

At the orphanage in Ocampo, Mexico, the sight of the children playing in the dirt courtyard put a lump in Jay's throat. Their poverty didn't dim their smiles when Jay and Oscar unloaded the boxes. Jay didn't require a translation for their shouts of *"Gracias!"*

"JOSÉ, THIS LAND is perfect for a church. How much is the seller asking?" Jay said as he studied the plot for sale in Ocampo.

"Three hundred fifty American dollars," José Gonzáles responded.

"I don't have that kind of money, but I can ask the churches back home to take up offerings to raise it," Jay said.

Later, with stationery and pen in hand, he hurried outside for better light. After he wrote five letters, Jay found Oscar. "Take me to the nearest post office?"

"Correos de México."

"Sí, los Correos de México," Jay said. "We need support from the States to build our first church."

"First?"

"Yes, first. My building background will come in handy."

Another day, Jay awoke, positive his dream came from the Lord. He dressed, then ran to find Oscar. Breathless, he grabbed his arm. "I've got news."

"News? From where?"

"From God."

"What?"

Jay ignored Oscar's incredulous look. "God gave me a dream. He wants me to build five hundred churches."

JAY ENTERED THE sanctuary early for his milestone service. He bowed at the altar. "Lord, give me the words . . ."

"Isaías cincuenta y cinco, seis—Busquen al Señor mientras puede ser hallado, llámenlo mientras está cerca . . . Isaiah 55:6, 'Seek ye the Lord while he may be found, call ye upon him while he is near.'"

After 3 years of mission work, Jay's calling had brought him to Paraguay, where he preached his first sermon in Spanish. The congregation's response thrilled him. He exited the newest church with the local pastor. "This is the best advice I have: Preach the gospel and pray. God will do the rest."

"Do you want joy and hope? Gather at our evening services and find the answers you seek," Jay said to the villagers. "Matthew 18:20 says, 'For where two or three are gathered together in my name, there am I in the midst of them.' Come meet Jesus, my friends. Don't wait until it's too late."

DEAR MISSIONS DIRECTORS,

Our work in Mexico, Paraguay, and Guatemala flourishes. We completed the fifth church, and it already overflows. As I'm only able to work on the mission field twice a year, please send more missionaries. Raise money to build more churches, and equip indigenous pastors to lead their people to Christ . . .

Jay set down the pen when his wife, CeCe, entered his home office in Biloxi, Mississippi. He watched her pace the small room.

"Another letter, Jay?"

"Yes, I have to write them, to gain support. This letter, though, is to the mission board. I want to get it in the mail before I leave for Guatemala tomorrow."

"It's too soon for you to go back. You're still recovering from a heart attack, for goodness' sake. You've been a missionary for 8 years. You deserve a rest," CeCe said.

"The Lord isn't done with me yet. There's too much to do," Jay told her.

"This is serious. It hasn't even been 2 months. We'll worry."

"I won't be gone as long this time. Another piece of land to see and a 2-week training session for new preachers, then I'll be home." Jay moved around the desk to stop CeCe's pacing. "Don't worry. Pray."

"I do pray, but . . ." CeCe crumpled into Jay.

Jay held her and kissed her temple. When CeCe recovered, he said, "Have faith, my love. God is with us."

JAY KNELT AT the altar of the new church in Jutiapa, Guatemala. After 16 years of missions, he felt more unworthy than ever. "Why did you choose me, Lord? The work is too big for me. I need You—"

"Brother Jay?" Pastor Mateo said as he entered the sanctuary.

Jay tried to rise but faltered.

"Let me help you, brother."

When Jay stood, he wobbled. "Help me sit. I'll be fine in a minute."

The pastor led him to a bench. "What day is it?"

"Thirty-eight, two more," Jay said.

"A forty-day fast. You've almost done it." Mateo chuckled. "I wouldn't last."

Jay didn't want to discuss the fast, and he hadn't—until people had begun to worry about his weight loss. "I may take a siesta. I find I enjoy them."

"Yes, the rest will do you good. The services are hard on you, but God is at work. I'm amazed at what He's doing."

"God is good. He's answering our prayers."

The fortieth night the Holy Spirit rested on Jay and strengthened him when he preached. Many cried out to Jesus. Jay stood back and watched the salvation of the Lord in awe.

JAY'S DAUGHTERS RUSHED to the visitor's desk at the New Orleans hospital. "Jay Matthews . . . flown in from Guatemala for emergency surgery." The volunteer checked her list, then pointed out the direction.

Jay awoke. His daughters and two missionary friends waited. He lifted his fingers in a wave, despite IV and oxygen tubes. His daughters rushed to his side and left wet patches on his shoulders, but he didn't care.

"Mama would be here if she could, Daddy," his oldest said.

"I know." Jay croaked. A younger daughter offered water. "Thank you."

"We have news, Brother Jay," his friend said.

"Yes, good news," the other said.

"You built the first church in 1969, right?" Jay nodded. "After almost 30 years, the number of churches you've helped build directly and indirectly has been tallied."

"Oh?"

"Yes, the total is . . . five hundred."

Jay's damaged heart leapt. His daughters grabbed tissues. "The Lord's timing is perfect. Many times I doubted His call, but the Lord is faithful. He carried me when I grew too weak or discouraged to continue. Praise God He let me live to see this. Five hundred churches, just in time. You did it, Lord. You did it!"

> Therefore I have reason to glory in Christ Jesus in the things which pertain to God.
>
> —Romans 15:17 (NKJV)

A time to
plant, and a time
to pluck up

THE UNFORESEEN CAREER CHANGE

— By Hannarich Asiedu —

MOST IMMIGRANTS COME to America in search of a better life. I was no exception. At twenty-five, the checklist for the life of my dreams seemed well underway. Completed my bachelor's degree? Check. Married to a dark, handsome man? Check. Working as head of employability and careers with a prestigious university in Ghana? Check. Evangelism secretary to my church? Check, check, check. And the icing on the cake—I had been granted conditional admission to a university in the United States of America. I had been looking forward to starting a combined master's and PhD program in public policy and political economy ever since I knew what it meant to have a career. I had long wanted to work with international humanitarian organizations, mainly the United Nations. After having worked a year with the United Nations Development Program (UNDP) right after my undergrad, it solidified my desire to continue that path.

Even though I had no funding for my study, I thought everything was possible in the United States of America, as many immigrants think before migrating. Surely, I would get funding somehow, some way. The Western world would have no struggles, only victories and glorious days, just like the way we see America portrayed on TV.

My husband and I arrived on a very cold, snowy day. Coming from Africa and having had absolutely no experience of this level of cold—or snow at all—it was a major challenge for us to adjust. But who cares? This was America; everything was possible, cold weather or not.

I studied and passed my GRE and was ready to apply for scholarships. I applied for almost a hundred of them. I got some responses, but nothing amounting to the thousands of dollars I would need to cover my student fees. From other institutions I got no responses at all. I had already started the semester, trying to find what work I could get as an international student and still looking everywhere possible for scholarships, but there were none.

I prayed. *God, where are You? Why are You not showing up? What happened to the favor I'm supposed to have in the sight of God and men, just like Jesus had* (Luke 2:52, NIV: "And Jesus grew in wisdom and stature, and in favor with God and man")? I had so much faith that my scholarship applications would succeed. Surely my faith was much bigger than a mustard seed, and yet, nothing. Sometimes "faith," it seems, is not enough. Or is it?

With no funding, I had to drop out of the program. I was heartbroken. All I had ever wanted, career-wise, was to complete my doctorate and continue working with international humanitarian organizations. Yet now here I was in the land of opportunities, the land where all dreams come true, and all my dreams were being shuttered right in front of me. My husband and I were going through the same difficulties—he also was not getting any scholarships for his studies, and with barely any income, our frustrations were overwhelming. *America isn't what we thought it would be. Should we go back home to Ghana?* We prayed fervently, and cried at times, but God didn't seem to care. Doors appeared permanently closed for us both.

> Truly I tell you, if you have faith as small as a mustard seed, you can say to this mountain, "Move from here to there," and it will move. Nothing will be impossible for you.
> —Matthew 17:20 (NIV)

A couple of years passed, with many other challenges, to the point that we almost became homeless because we had no jobs or money. Throughout that time, I constantly felt God prompting me to write. I loved to write, but never in my wildest imagination did I think of publishing anything. I did have a couple of ideas that God placed on my heart to write about, but surely that must be when I was retired from my career. Little did I know that God had a whole new career path for me.

But if writing was to be my path, write what, and how? I had no idea where to even begin looking. I took paid and free courses on writing, building a platform, and many other topics. Then, about 3 years after dropping out of the doctoral program, the answer to my prayers came. I met a young married lady who was preparing to have her first child, during which time her in-laws would move in with her for a couple of weeks. She was stressed because of the negative stereotypes she had seen and heard of in-law relationships. I wished that I could give her a book that I had written from my own experience—one that currently existed only in drafts—about attaining peaceful in-law relationships. I wasn't ready to finish that book, but God was. He put that urgency on my heart for the sake of this young wife who would benefit so much from my experience. The result was the draft of my first book, *Decoding the In-Law Code*.

After completing the draft, I knew I could either publish it myself independently or get a traditional publisher. I again felt the Holy Spirit leading me to submit book proposals and find a publisher. I thought because God Himself was asking me to get published traditionally, I would be accepted by the very first publisher I submitted my proposal to. Yet again, the rejections trickled in one after the other. I got hundreds of rejections. Why were none of the publishers and agents interested in contracting with me, although most indicated that they liked my work? I was frustrated. Why was God being so unkind? Was I doing something wrong? Was I not serving Him well enough? Was I not being kind to the poor, or even strangers? Was I not giving tithes and offerings enough? What did God want me to do before He finally came through?

Nothing, it seems; His timing and seasons are just different from ours. After hundreds of rejections of my book proposal from publishers and agents, I finally received interest in my manuscript from not one, but two publishers. The rejection period was over.

Not only did I sign my first book deal, but God also opened doors for me to speak, train, and coach. The main feedback I had from the publishers who rejected my book proposals was that I did not have a big enough platform. So, I soaked up as much information as possible about platform building and began putting these into practice immediately. I submitted articles as a guest blogger and spoke for free on my manuscript and other topics, hosted by groups on various platforms like Clubhouse, Facebook Live, YouTube, podcasts, and other venues. This opened me up to the world of speaking, coaching, and training.

I realized how much I enjoyed pouring knowledge into people with my words, either verbally or through my writings. This desire further led to my studying online and getting certified in the science of well-being under the instruction of cognitive scientist Dr. Laurie Santos at Yale University; as a life coach under applied psychologist Kain Ramsey; and later as a Chief Happiness

Officer under Woohoo Incorporated. In addition, the free writing, speaking, and training sessions led to paid opportunities that I hadn't anticipated for myself.

With my passion for humanitarian work, God led me to start supporting the philanthropy of others by connecting individuals and groups in the diaspora who were interested in volunteering in Africa to credible nonprofits. Our first volunteer, a retired engineer, would train young people who had previously been involved in illegal mining in rural communities in Ghana to give them employable skills in construction, solar panel installation, and more. I organized a book drive alongside my book launch and received several donations of books, crayons, and workbooks to help promote literacy in rural Ghana among children and young adults.

After many seasons of failures and rejections, God was now opening doors into brand-new territories. God was done tearing down my plans; He was now building His perfect plans through me.

Often, we don't realize that God's plans may not be the same as the plans we have for ourselves. We are shocked when our plans don't go as expected, and question whether God really answers prayers. And if He does answer them, are they answered too late? But God is always on time, and His plans are always perfect. Even when we go through seasons when we don't feel His presence, He is right there—ensuring some doors remain shut and opening new doors according to His perfect will.

A TIME AND WAY TO TEACH

— By Cathy Mayfield —

"**I DON'T WANT** to do school today! Do I have to?" The whiny sound of our five-year-old daughter's voice brought an echo from my memories.

"I don't want to go to school today!" I must have repeated that a hundred times over my school days, although not always aloud. From boredom to bullies, school was something to be avoided. I loved learning, though, and paid attention to lessons, did my homework, got A's on my tests. I enjoyed reading my textbooks, writing reports and essays, and even taking the achievement tests. Filling in those tiny boxes for my answers appealed to me and added to my desire to be a teacher someday. Even so, I hated the social parts necessary to make my dream come true.

After a tour of Millersville State Teacher's College in high school with my aunt and mentor, I figured my path to teaching in a public school was set. In a few years, I'd give assignments, teach grammar, and grade tests with the rest of the teachers.

Before graduation, though, I decided that my love for a boy superseded my desire for college, which, to be honest, terrified me because of my social ineptness. Kevin and I got married 1 year later, and he went to college. I assuaged my need for the school experience by helping him with his reports and lessons. With his

> For we are God's
> handiwork, created
> in Christ Jesus to do
> good works, which God
> prepared in advance
> for us to do.
> —Ephesians 2:10 (NIV)

technician's diploma, he found a job that allowed me to stay home while we started our family.

While waiting for our second daughter to arrive, Kevin and I began considering schooling options for the future. Public school hadn't fit us; neither of us liked the social scene or sports, which were big deals when we were in school. Someone mentioned homeschooling, which, though odd in 1986, still sounded interesting. But this was a few years before the Pennsylvania homeschool law, and no one I knew homeschooled their kids. I pushed off the idea, figuring it was a hoax. However, God had a plan.

Thirteen weeks before my due date, while on bedrest for 10 weeks with premature contractions, I forgot about anything but keeping my baby safe inside. A church friend of my mom's brought some magazines for me to read while resting. One had an article on homeschooling, reigniting the idea in my heart and making it real through the information.

After several years of phone calls, library visits, and attending an annual homeschool curriculum convention, I was set to be a teacher to two (and eventually, three) important students—our daughters. The year Holly, my oldest, turned four, I gathered the phonics program and math workbooks I'd purchased and set up our schoolroom. Old school desks my grandfather had found stood ready. And of course, yellow tablets and #2 pencils. My excitement grew by the minute.

On our planned first day, I looked around the room. A blackboard stood ready with chalk. An alphabet banner circled the wall. Early readers lay stacked on the table. I had a teacher's planning book and was ready to go.

However, several months later, our daughter protested as I woke her, "I don't want to do school today! Do I have to?"

What had happened? We read books every day, which she loved, and did projects, again things she loved. But she wasn't happy . . . and neither was I. I knew the phonics program bored her, as it did me. And the workbooks repeated things she already knew. But this was school! I had to teach rules and formulas, didn't I? And by then, our three-year-old daughter was begging to "do school" too. Would she react the same way?

At church one day, I cried out to God in frustration. "Father, You made me a teacher, so why isn't it working? I thought I knew how to teach, but I've made such a mess of it. I want so to be a good teacher for the girls. It shouldn't be hard. Please, show me how to teach Your way."

When I relayed our troubles to another homeschooling mom, she took me by the shoulders and said, "If you don't change, you're going to burn yourself and your girls out."

Change? I'd just prayed for God to show me His way to teach. Maybe teaching school at home wasn't really homeschooling. What if I incorporated me—my personality—into the teaching? But how? What part of me would make a difference?

For inspiration, I decided to visit a local teacher supply store. I looked at workbooks and charts. I found incentive pencils and erasers. I picked through a stock of reward stickers. Nothing different there—nothing "me."

I recalled my childhood years of learning crafts at my mother's side. She could take some toothpicks, grains of cat litter, and a milk cap and create a fire pit for a diorama. That was the part of me that I'd forgotten—creativity. I turned my search to unique and creative ideas for teaching.

> Whatever your hand
> finds to do, do it with
> all your might.
> —Ecclesiastes 9:10 (NIV)

On a shelf toward one side of the store, I found unit study books focused on teaching all the academic and nonacademic subjects around one topic. I remembered the joy we had with an endangered animals unit a teacher friend had given me. We'd read books about the diminishing habitat of pandas, did a math project on the plight of bald eagles, traced pictures of the large cats, like tigers and lions. It was creative and fun but educational in all subjects. That was my light-bulb moment: I had to find ways to make the learning process fun.

That day, I bought two unit studies, and the creative instincts God had given me went into overdrive. By the following year, I had planned two 9-week units with these books, complete with interactive bulletin boards and plenty of projects . . . and no phonics workbooks. The day before our first day of that school year, I looked at the displays of reading books and projects and knew I'd turned a corner. I would teach as I learned best—creating fun and education together.

One unit in my new curriculum included a bear hunt. While the girls and I made a trail mix, my husband went into the woods behind our house and hid several of the girls' stuffed bears in the trees. With paper-towel-tube binoculars and plastic bags of trail mix, we took a hike in the forest, singing the song, "The Bear Went over the Mountain." When the girls spied their bears, screams and giggles filtered through the trees and into my heart.

Over the years, creativity became a huge part of each day as I let go of schedules and textbooks. With the older two girls, we created a magazine of God's creature world, with short stories written by hand, spelled phonetically, and illustrated with traced pictures. The

English major in me closed her eyes at the atrocity of the writing. Ten years later, I helped our youngest with a "real" magazine—a sixteen-page, kitchen-table-published periodical called *Focus on Fun* for which she sold subscriptions. It covered the three Rs: reading (research), 'riting (stories, articles, puzzles), and 'rithmetic (finance math!).

At Christmastimes, we made gifts related to the unit study of the year. We made beaded bags while studying Native Americans and embroidered samplers during a unit set in colonial times. Eventually, the crafted items from various studies became displays in our local library.

So, yes, God helped me fulfill my long-held dream of becoming a teacher, but more importantly, He showed me *how* to teach—how to find that part of me that would eventually allow me to counsel and help other homeschoolers to find the unique fit for their own family dynamics.

The clincher came on a Monday holiday when I woke the girls and said, "No school today! It's Columbus Day!"

My heart did a giant flip when I heard, "But, Mommy, I want to do school today!"

A time to
plant, and a time
to pluck up

"TONY, TONY!"

— By Mary Bredel Fike —

IT WAS MAY. There was a feel of new life in the air. The kitchen curtains danced in the warm breeze passing through the window. I paused for a moment to look out and watch my husband, John, cutting the grass on the lower half of our hilly, 2-acre postage-stamp lot at the edge of my family's 200-acre farm.

Ah, the smell of just-mowed grass! I thought.

The crystal-blue sky, budding trees, and awakening perennial beds brought a sense of hope after the long winter. And my two-year-old daughter, Katie, falling asleep for her nap brought a sense of hope for a few quiet hours until my eight-year-old daughter, Jessica, would arrive home on the bus. I turned my attention back to my growing pile of paperwork.

The monotonous drone of the riding lawnmower came to an abrupt stop. I went back to the window.

My husband was lying on the ground with both hands reaching under the mower deck trying to remove the buildup of moist grass.

"Thank You, God, that he remembered to turn off the mower!" I made my way back to the kitchen counter.

No sooner had I sat down than I heard the mower start up again, just briefly, then stop. I looked out the window.

Why is he holding his hands? Oh, God, I hope he didn't cut his fingers.

I hurried out onto the deck. He slowly walked up the hill staring down at his cupped hands.

"Honey, what's wrong? Did you cut your hand?" I asked.

"I don't know what happened," he said.

"Is your hand okay?" I didn't see any blood.

"It's not my hand; I thought I put it in a safe place. I can't believe it happened. I can't believe I lost my wedding ring."

I reached for his grass-stained hands; they were trembling. The ring was gone.

"I'm sure we can find it," I said. "Do you know exactly where you were when you think you lost it?"

"Probably by the pile of wet grass I cleaned out. How did it roll off the seat?"

As soon as Jessica came home from school, she was given the assignment to keep an eye on her sister. John and I walked the lower yard back and forth in equal distances from the spot he had described.

"I can't believe I did this," John said. "I was so glad the yard was almost done! It's gotta be here somewhere."

Overly exhausted from pacing and tracing our steps, and faced with the sun lowering in the sky, we came to an agreement: stop for now and start again tomorrow.

John recruited his coworker and her brother, who had a military-grade metal detector, to join our search party. They came late the next day and two times after and traced John's path. Back and forth they went, methodically surveying the backyard. Their results? A few erroneous beeps.

"Oh, Saint Anthony, help us!" I said.

"Why him?" John asked.

"He's the patron saint of lost things. I remember a friend who always prayed, 'Tony, Tony, come around. Something's lost and can't be found,' when she lost things."

"Did it work?"

"Sometimes. You have to have faith. God knows where it is. We'll keep looking and praying."

"Where could it have gone?"

"You never know," one friend said to us later. "Sometimes a crow will pick up shiny objects and carry them away."

Another "helpful" suggestion we heard: "You probably kicked it down into the hay field with the blades. You'll probably never find it."

John wasn't ready to give up. Whenever we walked the bottom of the yard, we took the time to look and see if maybe—just maybe—we would find it. I felt so bad for John.

"It just feels strange without the ring on my finger," he said.

"You know, we can take some solace that it is planted in our property or my parents'. It's a part of us," I said.

"It's not just a part; it's my wedding ring. It's a symbol of our marriage, and it's gone."

"John, we have each other and two beautiful daughters, our faith, and our health."

FIVE YEARS LATER, I decided to surprise John with a new ring for our fifteenth wedding anniversary. Our daughters were in on my surprise. Before I picked them up at their parochial school, I made a quick stop at the jewelry store and purchased a ring similar to the one he lost.

"Shouldn't we get the ring blessed, like they do in weddings?" the girls asked.

"I don't think Father is here this afternoon," I said.

"Oh, who needs Father. We can do it!" Katie said. "We wouldn't be here if there wasn't a wedding. Who better than us?"

The girls rushed toward the church and together pushed the large wooden doors open. They were jockeying for the best position next to the holy water font when I caught up to them.

"We'll bless it good, Mom, real good. Just watch us," Jessica said.

I handed the silver ring to the girls, and they proceeded to carefully dip it in the holy water font, accompanied by a few giggles and prayers. Only God knew what was in their hearts.

After we arrived home, the girls sat at the kitchen counter and did their homework. I was preparing dinner.

"Mom, do we have to wait until dinner?" Jessica asked. "Can't you give it to him now, puh-lease?"

"What's all the commotion?" John asked as he walked into the kitchen. (Secrets are hard to keep with two young daughters.)

"Mom has a surprise. Just wait," Katie said.

I gently placed a small black velvet box in the palm of John's left hand.

"Would you marry me?" I asked.

"Come on, come on, Dad. Open it and answer the question," Katie said.

"Yes, yes," John said. His face lit up as he carefully lifted the lid. "Oh my . . . it looks exactly like my ring."

"Yeah, and don't lose this one, Dad," the girls said.

MANY YEARS PASSED, and another May arrived. John still had the ring, but time had taken its toll on us in other ways. My struggles with lupus had forced me to retire nearly two decades before. John had recently become a retiree himself after Parkinson's disease started to interfere with his work.

I was sitting with John on the deck in the early sunlight while enjoying our coffee. Looking out at the garden, I began to tear up. John looked at me. "What's bothering you?" he asked.

"There's so much work to do in the garden. It's going to be such a challenge," I said. "But honey, I can't let lupus take away my gardening. I feel so close to God when I'm gardening, feeling the warmth of the soil and watching things grow."

"What if we scale things down?" John asked. "I'll help you. I'm not working."

"Could we plant a butterfly garden by the woods? Not too big, but I do have a few dill volunteer plants I could move by myself. Swallowtails love them."

After we finished our coffee, John left to clear a small spot for me close to the house where I could transplant the dill. I was leaving the garage with my gardening tools when John returned to the house.

"Do you need help?" he asked.

"No, thanks," I said. "I'll take my time and rest."

"Well, I'll be cutting the grass. Just holler for me."

"Don't worry. I'm with the Master Gardener!"

Three trips up and down a slight grade later, I was running out of energy. After I pressed another dill weed into the dirt, I sat on the soft grass, trying to enjoy the warmth of the sun coming from the east. Frustrated by my limitations, I began to question God.

I know You have all things in Your divine plan, but why? The girls are grown; I have time to garden and can't. It's such a struggle.

I was ready to pull off my dirty gloves and call it quits for the morning when I felt a divine nudge. I needed to move just one more dill.

Slowly I made my way up to the garden and back. The dill roots were intact. Now the decision of a perfect spot remained.

I noticed the bright noon sun illuminating the base of a small tree at the edge of the cleared spot. I grasped a clump of grass, which yielded with a gentle pull.

> Those who sow in tears will reap with cries of joy.
> —Psalm 126:5 (NABRE)

"Perfect."

I slid my hand shovel into the dark humus soil to the length of the six-inch blade. I lifted the shovel to turn over the soil. Something shiny caught my eye.

I immediately laid the shovel down.

"Oh, my God. Oh my." My hands began to shake. "This can't be. This spot is so far away and up the hill! It can't be possible. Tony, Tony, thank you! I guess the prayer never specified a time frame. Oh, thank you, Saint Anthony. It must be over 20 years!"

I gently pushed the packed dirt away.

"Unbelievable. It's perfect."

John passed a few feet away on the mower.

"John!" I yelled. He quickly turned the mower off. "Come quick. Hurry," I said.

"Are you okay?" John asked as he saw me holding my hands tightly.

"Oh, yes. Oh, yes. Just wait. First, I have a question: Would you marry me?"

"What are you talking about?"

"You'll see; just wait. Hold out your left hand and close your eyes."

"What's going on?"

"Just do it."

As he closed his eyes, I gently clasped his left hand and carefully laid on his palm the long-lost wedding ring.

CHAPTER
2

BREAKING DOWN AND BUILDING UP

ECCLESIASTES 3:3

A time to kill,
and a time to heal;
a time to break down,
and a time to build up

INTRODUCTION

Stories of breaking down, "killing" the things they needed to be rid of, and then healing and building themselves back up

— By Shirley Raye Redmond —

CAPTAIN EDDIE RICKENBACKER (1890–1973) was one of the most extraordinary heroes of the twentieth century and a legend in his own time. Strong-willed and ambitious, Captain Eddie—as he would be called for most of his life—loved engines. He loved speed. He became one of America's earliest professional race car drivers, eventually owning and operating the Indianapolis Motor Speedway for 20 years.

But he is perhaps best known for his exploits as a pilot during World War I. After joining General Pershing's American Expeditionary Forces, he was sent to France, where he soon worked his way into the Air Service. After only 17 days of training, Eddie took to the skies.

By his own count, Eddie survived one hundred and thirty-five brushes with death during his adventurous lifetime. Perhaps the most amazing took place during World War II when Captain Eddie, employed as a civilian, served as a special consultant for Secretary of War Henry Stimson. In 1942, Eddie was a civilian passenger aboard a military plane that ran out of gas while trying to locate a tiny refueling station in the Pacific Ocean. The pilot ditched the plane. Eddie and six other men spent 24 days stranded in the ocean on three small rubber life rafts before being rescued. One man died of exposure.

A crew member with a small New Testament and Psalms in his pocket would occasionally read from it. With the men nearer and nearer to death, Captain Eddie decided it was a good time to share his Christian faith with the others, which he did. He also suggested they hold a prayer meeting each day, insisting all the men participate, whether they were believers or not. The little book was passed around, and each man read a passage. Sometimes it was a favorite psalm or perhaps a familiar chapter in the Gospels. Other times, someone would simply open the pages at random and read the verses on that page. The men sang hymns. They prayed. Soon, they began to confess their sins to one another. They shared their hopes and dreams and fears.

On the eighth day after holding prayer meetings, things changed. Rickenbacker mentioned in his autobiography that on that day a small miracle occurred. A seagull landed on his head. Snatching it quickly, Eddie wrung its neck and shared the food carefully among the starving men. They chewed the morsels slowly, savoring each bite. They used the entrails to catch fish. When it began to rain, Eddie caught the precious drops of fresh water in his hat for all to share. Soon, a plane flew overhead. They waved frantically, and they were spotted and ultimately rescued. When retelling the incident years later, Captain Eddie admitted there were those who said it was all a coincidence, but he declared it was a gift from heaven.

IN EDDIE RICKENBACKER we have someone who killed during the course of war and brought healing to his crewmates in desperate situations, who was broken down and then built himself back up over the course of a long career. Likewise, many of the people whose stories you'll read in the following chapter have been through times when they were broken down—by addiction, by mourning, by challenges that seemed overwhelming—and with God's grace built themselves back up. You'll read stories of addiction and recovery, bitterness and forgiveness, and how God's plans for us so often are much bigger than those we make for ourselves.

DREAMING WITH GOD

— By Roberta Messner —

I SAT IN a circle of seventeen participants at my pain management support group. "I have a challenge for everyone," our petite, dark-haired psychologist announced. "If you could accomplish anything, and you knew you could not fail, what would that be?" Her eyes surveyed the group, all of whom wore years of chronic pain on their weary faces. Her warm voice beckoned someone—anyone—to join in the conversation.

As a registered nurse, I'd led my own share of groups. Recognized that awkward silence too. When everyone stared silently at the beige tile floor, I heard a voice that sounded like mine say, "Okay, I'll go first.

"For those who don't know me, I've suffered from agonizing tumor pain since I was an infant," I said. "I've had thirty-seven surgeries, but the tumors always win, returning bigger and more invasive than before."

The psychologist's eyes found mine, urging me to go on. I explained how two decades before, when the drug OxyContin came on the market, my physician christened it perfect for me. It made life more bearable for a while. Eventually, it stole everything from that life when I became addicted to it. "When the opioid epidemic hit, my insurance stopped paying for my medication. So I ended up here for other options."

How will you ever make it, Roberta? I'd panicked. The nerve pain felt like searing, hot coals were pressed to my eyes and face. Pain and its sidekicks—fatigue and discouragement—had choreographed most of my 63 years. When I'd had my first tumor removed as a child, the surgeon cautioned my mother: "Don't get your hopes up. Those nerve cells have a memory like an elephant. They never forget the pain."

In the welcoming acceptance of the group, I admitted something I'd never told another soul. "I know exactly what I'd change, but I *can* fail. I *have* failed. Over and over in my mind, though I've never tried to do it."

"What's that, Roberta?" the psychologist asked. There was no judgment in her voice, only caring. Her compassion moved into every cell of my body.

"Well, I live in this ramshackle log cabin," I said. "It's over a hundred years old and needs a ton of work." I couldn't spit out the most important part. My eyes locked with a fellow nurse who'd lost her beloved home in the madness of opioid dependence. "My cabin?" I said. "I once had dreams for the two of us. There's this big, light-filled space, but it's crammed floor to ceiling with stuff I found junking. Big plans for that stuff, too. Know what I'd love? To carve me a nurturing place. But pain has flat wore me out. I'm too exhausted to take on such a thing."

The psychologist stressed it was fine to ask for help with such matters. Who was she kidding? I'd isolated myself from everyone. Besides, I'd never find anyone willing to take that—or me—on. It was utterly hopeless. I hadn't been able to even pray lately.

One night as sleep eluded me, a strength welled up inside me; from where, I did not know. I dared to do the impossible. Told God about my dream and boldly asked Him to send me such a person.

Two days later, the most preposterous thing happened. A consignment shop called to say they were cleaning their storage

> Take delight in the
> LORD, and he will
> give you the desires
> of your heart.
> —Psalm 37:4 (NIV)
>
> ∾

area and had run into something I'd purchased years before. It all came back to me. The once-upon-a-time October day I'd believed in possibilities. The sweet, honey-pine farm table I'd snared for a song. It even had those white porcelain casters I'd always adored. But it had been too big to fit into my vehicle, so they'd agreed to put it in storage for me. When pain and those opioids took over my life, I'd forgotten all about it.

"We'll bring that table right to your home," the lady was now offering. "No trouble at all. I have an angel of a delivery guy." The next morning, a man with shoulder-length gray hair pulled into a ponytail and wearing a bandana sweatband appeared at my door. He didn't look like anyone dispatched from heaven, but when he muscled my table up the stone steps, I began to wonder.

If Brett was an angel, he sure was a bold one. When he stepped inside, he let out a long whistle. "What in tarnation happened here?" he asked as his eyes surveyed the log walls. "This is prime real estate. Do you know how incredible it could be? You need to *live* in this space."

My eyes took in the mismatched chairs lining the walls. They looked like dear friends gathered for a reunion, awaiting my honey-pine table. An antique dry sink I'd found curbside on trash day. I'd been drawn to the beautifully worn discards like a bug to light. There was a door with a chippy-paint finish I'd dumpster-dived for, back when I could dive. What if I kitty-cornered it and hung a wreath to welcome . . . me?

It was all the stuff of dreams. I only needed a dream-maker.

You may have guessed the next part of my story. Brett was a master reinventor who made it all happen. The two of us took my would-be treasures and turned them into a nurturing space. While we were scheming, he told me how he'd once traveled the world as a chef. "When my health took a downward turn, that dream died," he said. "Now I stay close to home and help people like you."

We worked outside on pretty days and used the lawn for stations—keep, toss, donate, sell, give away. He fixed me a seat and brought each item for me to evaluate. The two of us agreed on just about everything until I pronounced my ancient wing chair a keeper. "*This one?*" he asked incredulously, eyeing the straw stuffing popping through its ragged upholstery. "It's beyond redemption."

Now I was the bold one. "When I happened onto this baby, I was tickled to bits," I countered. "Got it for next to nothing." I patted its tall back, perfect for a contemplative headrest. "Solid wood construction. Hand-tied springs. Great lines. They don't make 'em like that anymore."

"I've heard of reverence for the reimagined," he quipped. "But that frosts the ol' carrot cake." I could hear an edge of amusement in his voice.

As the space cleared, something outside myself began to happen. Settling into my nest of comfort, order, and beauty, a marvelous energy filled my body. God Himself was there. He really was there—in a tumbledown log cabin that needed fixing up as much as its owner.

The project took all summer and fall, but I sold enough stuff to pay for the new improvements. I sent a couple of vintage advertising signs home with Brett so he'd always remember his angelic assignment and my deep gratitude.

In the months that followed, an unfathomable dream came true. A pain management specialist determined a new medication might better control my torment. I experienced a harrowing withdrawal from the opioids but was buoyed by an Unseen Force. Behind the scenes, friends and strangers stormed heaven on my behalf, with no idea of what they were even praying for. There is no earthly explanation for what happened, only that the change in meds was so shocking to my brain, it somehow reprogrammed me. From that day forward, I have had no tumor pain nor the need or the slightest craving for the meds that once controlled my life.

Those time-tattered comments about nerve pain and its relentless memory had outlived their usefulness. Just like those opioids and all that junk I'd discarded.

These days, I begin each day by brewing a pot of tea. I snuggle into my refurbished ancient wing chair, its straw stuffing now well secured. Open God's Word and meditate instead of medicate. As I close my eyes, I marvel that it's no longer just the two of us . . . a century-old log cabin and Roberta. There are three now, and God's dreams are bigger than anything I could imagine. In the distance, I hear the tinkling of a teacup, pages turning in a well-worn Bible. It is the sound of my own heart.

**A time to
kill, and a
time to heal**

MILK ALLERGY MIRACLE

— By Rebecca Borger —

I STOOD NEXT to my KitchenAid mixer, one hand pressed to the top, the other carefully pouring powdered milk into the bowl. Moving the lever to the lowest setting, I started the mixer, stirring the milk powder into the flour. The dry mixture puffed up a little into the air, and I sucked in a breath. My knuckles blanched white as I gripped the mixer, body tense and on high alert as my 18-year-old son, Asher, walked by. We were days away from moving him to college, and he was striding back and forth through the kitchen, gathering items for school. I was preparing what would become his daily dose of baked milk while away, a treatment for his potentially fatal milk allergy. It was the first time in more than 18 years I had poured a milk product in our house—let alone a dry product that could waft in the air, to be inhaled by our son's vulnerable lungs. I watched as he passed by, my eyes filling with tears. He was fine. Totally fine. No allergic reaction. No issue whatsoever. I couldn't believe I was pouring powdered milk inside my house, inside the mixer, into the very air he would breathe. But, in fact, I was. I never thought this day would come. This is the story of his healing.

Within weeks of Asher's birth, we knew something unusual was happening. His skin was red as though he had a sunburn, and he often seemed congested. He would break out in hives. Scary reactions and health events began to occur. By the time he was nine months old, we had the full diagnosis: multiple, life-threatening food allergies along with reactive airway disease, which would develop into full-fledged asthma as he grew. His biggest food allergen was milk. The milk allergy paired with the asthma diagnosis meant that exposing him to dairy products could produce a fatal, multisystem reaction. We were about to embark on a journey of living with a life-threatening milk allergy. It would be more socially isolating than we could imagine; it would change the way we lived our lives.

As the years went by, we worked hard as a family to create a warm environment with delicious foods. All new family recipes, dairy free and nut free. An entire Thanksgiving feast with everything safe. Birthday cakes, Christmas cookies, holiday celebrations, Saturday night pizza: memories made around the table in a space where he could eat freely and enjoy. Grocery shopping remained a careful, tedious process: read every label every time. Without warning, safe family staples would disappear from the store or change ingredients. Bread that had always been milk-free suddenly wasn't. The dairy-free sour cream we always used was no longer available or very hard to find. And on and on.

Worst of all, perhaps, were the prescription medicines. One year, we had pneumonia go through the family. Asher ended up having a frightening allergic reaction to the milk protein in the prescribed antibiotic; he was vomiting and had difficulty breathing, with swollen lips and deep red skin. It was our allergist who helped us unearth what was causing the reaction, and I had to call the drug manufacturer to determine what we already knew from the witness of his body: there was milk protein among the undisclosed ingredients. The amount of milk in the antibiotic was trace. The difficulty breathing caught me off guard because he was sick with pneumonia. The experience was a terrifying reality check.

Allergic reactions to milk always included difficulty breathing, asthma, hives, extreme congestion, itching, a general feeling of illness, and other varying symptoms, depending on exposure. He had to carry epinephrine, Benadryl, and rescue inhalers everywhere.

Now faith is the assurance of things hoped for, the conviction of things not seen.

—Hebrews 11:1 (ESV)

Every now and again, I would read a post or article from someone whose life had been changed by a medical process called Oral Immunotherapy (OIT), which involves gradually building up tolerance to an allergen through controlled doses. We learned that Johns Hopkins in Baltimore, Maryland, was at the forefront of this research for milk allergy. I tucked that information away, desiring to keep aware of allergy advances while living life as best we could.

Providentially, after many years, my husband had a job offer in Maryland, very close to Johns Hopkins. It was a top hospital in the nation for food allergy care and research, and even aside from the OIT research, our son would benefit from the experts found there. We took a leap of faith and managed the move just as the calendar year turned from 2012 to 2013. Asher was ten. We settled in, got him established at Johns Hopkins at their pediatric allergy and immunology clinic, and found out that there were no current OIT research studies in progress. The one I had read about hadn't had the success they expected, and things were on hold.

Homeschooled for personal conviction (not because of food allergies), Asher played soccer at the local Christian school and participated in Boy Scouts. He navigated restaurants on away game nights, sometimes having to step outside because of airborne allergies or deal with close contact reactions. He always packed his own food everywhere he went. We would prepare and bring all of his food to Scout camp so that he could participate like everyone else. We never went to a restaurant as a family. Every social event was a landmine of potential danger, from the milk in a baby's bottle or toddler cup to the cupcake in a friend's hand or the pizza after the game. During his junior year of high school, I watched as, after one of the last soccer games of the season, the team launched full gallons of liquid milk high into the air to crash down on the grassy lawn beside the field near where he was sitting. Everyone knew of his allergy. I couldn't understand why anyone would do something so dangerous around him.

When Asher was a junior in high school, a milk research study for oral immunotherapy opened. This study was for children who could not tolerate baked milk, who needed to be in a medically supervised environment, and who met certain criteria for severe milk allergy. Our son was placed in the lottery. When his name finally came up, he had a hard decision to make. There were no guarantees the oral immunotherapy would work; he would be taking a life-threatening risk every day. However, there was also the hope of how his life might transform if the study did work. In the end, he decided to enter the study, quietly and without fanfare, trusting the Lord. That night, we praised God for the answer to our prayers and our step of faith so many years before.

For the trial, he had to ingest a medically determined, precise dose of baked milk protein every day. He took this in the form of a cupcake. After certain periods of time, this dose would be carefully increased. Over the course of the year, Asher endured some serious reactions, especially when up-dosing to the next level. We had several frightening middle-of-the-night experiences where we had to make judgment calls as to how serious the situation actually was. Was it just Benadryl and inhalers or did we need to use the EpiPen?

He did make it through the entire year without the need for epinephrine. But meanwhile, the baked milk caused his eczema to flare significantly, and we were treating skin issues with creams and prescriptions.

But for you who fear my name, the sun of righteousness shall rise with healing in its wings.

—Malachi 4:2 (ESV)

Even though it was difficult, that first year was a success. Looking at my husband at the end of year one, the doctor said, "Next year, he will be able to eat a piece of pizza." It was a shocking statement for both of us. It felt so out of this world. How could this be?

The next year was his senior year of high school; we were preparing for his next steps. We reached out to one of his doctors about college dining hall navigation, and she told us that cross-contamination from milk wasn't going to be a problem for him anymore. I didn't believe her. Doctors had given me wrong information before, and I had spent so many years living with the reality that my son was allergic, severely allergic to milk. I didn't want to get my hopes up. Also, although he was in the study and consuming a medical dose of baked milk every day, the rest of our life had to stay the same. Protocol demanded we not change anything. We continued on just as we always had: avoiding milk and taking every precaution. We toured the dining hall at his future school and were relieved by the allergen protocols the school had in place.

Just weeks before Asher was to move into his freshman dorm, he completed the exit challenge for the food allergy research study. He had been in the study for more than 2½ years at that point. Before my eyes, he consumed three-quarters of a small frozen pizza prepared according to the doctor's guidelines. He was eating real cheese! As the doctor watched, he looked me right in the eye and said, "You will never have to worry about cross contamination again." Tears spilled down my cheeks. I thought about all the allergy alerts I would never ever have to fear again. The constant worry for Asher's safety lifted in one unbelievable moment.

IT WAS MOVE-IN week, and we were hours from leaving Asher settled at school. We purposely got lunch at a deli he would eat at during orientation, wanting to give him a comfortable reference point for ordering and navigating the experience on his own. We sat down at the table with sandwiches toasted in butter and cross contaminated with cheese. He took a crispy bite, his eyes widening with surprised enjoyment. "Wow, this tastes good!"

I stared at the miracle before my eyes, overwhelmed with gratitude. God be praised!

We made a move of faith in 2013, never knowing how perfectly the Lord would provide the answer to our prayers: the trial ended successfully in the summer of 2021, right before Asher was scheduled to move away and eat daily from a dining hall where we couldn't control his exposure to allergens. Not only that, but the Lord made a way for him, through OIT, to be safe in social settings that previously would have been very dangerous for him, allowing him to socially integrate into all aspects of college life. God was in the hard, dark times and in the miraculous, joyous light. This healing remains to this day beyond our wildest dreams.

A time to
kill, and a
time to heal

THE RESILIENCY OF A COFFEE MUG AND A LITTLE GIRL

— By Laurie Davies —

HOW DID YOU survive? I thought, clasping the coffee mug in both hands before tossing it into the dumpster. *I barely did.*

The last time I'd seen that mug, a backhand from my dad had sent us both airborne, spilling coffee and innocence onto the floor.

"No," I said, the single syllable breaking as I quickly swiped away tears. I wouldn't be losing my composure today. I had work to do. My dad had just passed away, and his landlord needed to turn his apartment over.

I PLAYED IN the basement while my dad did important work at his big desk. Mindful of being quiet, I poked colored pegs into my Lite-Brite, delighted each time a new color illuminated the black paper pattern and my six-year-old world. "Honey, please go upstairs and get me coffee," my dad said, distractedly motioning backward with his mug. "Don't spill."

I'd never been asked to do an important job like this before. My dad's tone sounded safe, and it seemed like it was going to be a good day.

51 • Breaking Down and Building Up

I bounded up the stairs to the kitchen, carefully poured coffee, and sidestepped down the stairs, one at a time, both hands clasped around the mug. I was so proud of myself for not spilling a drop. Those steps were steep, and my legs were little.

I took the coffee to my dad, and he took a big swig.

In an instant, I was airborne, literally knocked off my feet from the force of my dad's hand.

Lukewarm coffee. That's all it took to provoke him to violence.

I still can't figure out the physics. How were the mug and I airborne at the same time? Why didn't that mug shatter when it hit the hard basement floor? Why didn't I? In a childhood blurry from trauma, how is it possible that I remember the sharp outline of streaks of coffee racing me through the air?

"HEY, YOU OKAY?" My husband jolted me to the present as I walked inside to get another heavy box of memories.

"Yeah, I'm good." My stiff upper lip didn't fool him; he'd been reading the subtext in my face for 20 years.

"We'll get through this, you know. You're going to be okay," he said, maneuvering a bookcase outside.

Maybe the bedroom is a better place to work, I thought, pulling clothing from hangers. I'd make three piles: keep, donate, throw away. "There's that awful Hawaiian shirt," I said, disarmed by a funny memory of my own adult banter with my dad over his questionable fashion sense. When Dad wanted to be the life of the party, he was. He was gregarious and hilarious, willing and able to command any room. His personality was as big as he was tall, and his 6-feet-1 height meant that, in my family of shorter men, the "keep" pile was empty.

Almost everything would be tossed or donated, especially that outlandish Hawaiian shirt. "Someone else can embarrass their children with this," I said, allowing the memory to pry my stiff upper lip into a smile.

> For I am about to do something new. See, I have already begun!
> —Isaiah 43:19 (NLT)

I reached into the corner to grab one final item, this one sealed away in a heavy garment bag. I unzipped it, half expecting to find the suit he wore when he sat in the back at my wedding. He'd been an invited guest and yet a spectator—the father of the bride who watched the maternal grandfather of the bride give her away. I'd heard he'd been choked up that day, leaving before the ceremony was over. He sent a lovely gift with a note of gratitude for the invitation.

I lugged the bag outside and unzipped it to find my dad's United States Marine Corps uniform. "Oh, Dad," I whispered. "There's so much about you I don't know."

My dad came home from Vietnam a hard man. Who knows, maybe he went there a hard man. He never talked about his military service. I wasn't sure what the colored ribbons above the left pocket meant, but the rifle sharpshooter badge told me he had been trained to view men as targets. That's an uncompromising way to look at people.

Another tear escaped my eye, and I let this one fall. I zipped the garment bag and carefully started a "keep" pile.

THERE WOULD BE no chance for closure, because my dad was gone. There could only be healing. I prayed God would help me get to one without the other. On one hand, I felt sad that my dad hadn't been able to lower his guard enough to seek the forgiveness

> I will take out
> your stony,
> stubborn heart and
> give you a tender,
> responsive heart.
> –Ezekiel 36:26 (NLT)
>
> ∼

I would have willingly given. On the other hand, I felt the Lord compelling me to forgive anyway.

I didn't want to walk through life with "daddy issues," a phrase I'd always found casually unfunny. I didn't want to walk with a limp. People in my life needed me to be whole. On this hardest of days, God began to answer my prayer for healing, giving me the desire to forgive my dad.

I stepped outside to place a tough telephone call, telling a family member the news of my dad's passing. I nervously tried to soften the news by offering to send photos from a small box I'd found. "Do you want one, maybe from high school?" I asked, sure that happier memories of my dad existed further back on his timeline. "I found one of him in his football uniform."

I learned in that conversation that my dad was a high-school football star. He loved football. His height, physique, and explosiveness gave him an edge, but there was one thing he didn't have on game days.

His dad.

I learned from someone else that day that his dad never attended a single one of his games. I never met my paternal grandfather, but I knew he was an important petroleum industry executive. What I hadn't known was that his relationship with his son had been combustible, too.

As I carefully placed the photo on the "keep" pile, I reached back in time to mourn for a boy whose dad didn't come watch him play the sport he loved. I pictured my dad's million-dollar smile—perhaps held back slightly by wistfulness—when his coach was the one to say, "You were good out there tonight, Jimmy."

In my dad's death, I started to form a different composite from the one I'd allowed myself to create in his life. I saw him suiting up in pads that absorbed football tackles, but not the deeper injuries. I saw him as a marine corporal, trained to shoot anyone who didn't look like him. I saw him in that awful Hawaiian shirt, relishing the attention that he needed maybe more than I knew. I saw him as a man who watched someone else give his daughter away. I imagined him working in a dark, dank basement with all that pain unattended and unhealed.

I had come to empty my dad's apartment, but the bitterness I'd nurtured for years began to leak out instead. It was never okay for my dad to take his pain out on those he was supposed to protect. But I also didn't want to entertain a hard heart toward him anymore.

The first ripples of healing were layering onto the edges of my story.

IN A LITERAL sense, I live in a valley—the metropolitan area I call home is nicknamed the Valley of the Sun. The irony that the weekend's work took place in northern Arizona's mountains wasn't lost on me.

It's not usually the descent back down into the valley I long for. I want the mountaintop experience—a weekend revelation, just like the one I'd received about forgiving my dad. But the lasting work of healing doesn't happen on the mountaintop, at least not for me. My healing with my dad would get worked out in the valley, in everyday decisions to lather empathy onto shattered pieces of the past.

It wouldn't happen overnight, and it wouldn't be easy. But those were details I didn't need to know yet. I drove my SUV, with its small "keep" pile—items that, over time, would become markers of my own softened, healed heart toward my dad—down the 4,000-foot descent to the desert floor. I knew that God had given me life there. I knew He wanted me to *live*. And I knew healing—a real kind of healing that reflects the Healer—was ahead.

A time to break
down, and a time
to build up

I DIDN'T SIGN UP FOR THIS

— By Janet Paige Smith —

"LOCK ON TARGET!" I shouted to the soldiers packed inside
the fire control van as I prepared to launch a long-range missile.

My fingers trembled above the red button penetrating the inky
black darkness of the van. Sweat dripped down my face from under
my helmet.

"Target in range, Lieutenant," said my platoon sergeant as he
watched his radar screen.

"On my command . . . 5 . . . 4 . . ." Seconds later, the missile
launched and the target disappeared. The van erupted in cheers as
hands patted me on the back.

When I stepped outside the van, my commanding officer smiled
and gave me a handshake. "Congratulations, Lieutenant Smith," he
said. "You are the first female officer to launch a long-range missile
in the United States." My tears flowed freely. This time I didn't care
if my soldiers saw me cry. The year was 1981, and I'd just overcome
the odds to make history.

THREE MONTHS EARLIER, I had driven the long stretch of
highway that divided the shimmering sands of New Mexico on the

way to McGregor Range, my first assignment as a second lieutenant in the army. A soldier waved me through the security checkpoint. I entered the army outpost where the only active Nike Hercules missile in the country was located. I parked in front of the narrow, tan, concrete-block headquarters for the 2/52nd Air Defense Artillery Battalion, one of several structures built close together like row houses. This cluster of buildings was where my soldiers slept, ate, and spent their free time. They called it "The Middle of Nowhere."

Sweat rolled down my back, not only from the desert heat, but from the thought of reporting to my commanding officer. Yesterday, I'd seen him observing me during morning formation.

"Platoon! Attention!" I ordered. The command should have prompted them to shift position, standing straight, feet together, and perfectly still, awaiting further orders. Instead, soldiers shuffled their feet, rolled their eyes, even chuckled. I gave the command again. I was nervous, and my voice sounded like I was yelling instead of giving orders. The soldiers grumbled, but came to attention. They knew just how far to push me without showing disrespect.

After work, the commanding officer told me to come and see him in the morning.

The next day, I reported as ordered. Smoothing out the winkles in my uniform, I entered the cool building, knocked, opened the door, and stood at attention in front of his desk.

"Lieutenant," he said, "since you've been assigned here, your men have had a hard time following your orders. Your platoon is performing below average, and several of your soldiers have gotten into trouble."

"Sir, let me explain," I said.

"Don't bother," he said. "I expect rowdy conduct out of your younger soldiers, but your Vietnam war veterans are mature and

> Be strong and
> courageous, because
> you will lead these
> people . . .
> —Joshua 1:6 (NIV)
>
> ∿

experienced. We are in a cold war with the Soviet Union. Our battery will launch a practice missile in three months. I need your soldiers—and you—ready."

"Yes, sir!" I said fighting the sting of tears.

Outside his office, my shoulders sagged. He was right. I had thought my soldiers would respect me with time, but things had gotten worse.

After leaving the headquarters building, I drove 4 more miles through the desert toward the fire control van where my soldiers and I spent our days. The van sat on a large concrete slab surrounded by humming generators that emitted gas fumes into the desert air. Two olive-drab metal buildings, each the size of a hut, sat nearby. One was my office; the other, where the soldiers took their breaks from the sweltering sun. Farther out into the desert stood a Nike Hercules missile, pointed upward like a skyscraper. In the background lay the beautiful Sacramento Mountains. Their presence wrapped peace around the missile that waited, ready to destroy.

On the way home that evening, discouraged by my inability to lead my soldiers, I began to doubt my decision to join the Army. I'd been in the Reserve Officers' Training Corps (ROTC) at the University of Georgia, but giving orders to a group of college cadets while marching around a parking lot was like kids playing army compared to the reality of leading soldiers.

When my ROTC instructor called me into his office my senior year and asked me if I wanted to become an air defense officer, I said, "No." I had majored in social work and envisioned myself sitting in an office, counseling families. But his recruiting pitch was too good to turn down. He told me I'd start in a leadership position and travel the world. If I didn't like the Army, I could leave in 3 years. Now, after 3 months, I didn't know if I'd last the year.

At home, I called my dad, a retired sergeant, for advice. He had supported my decision to join the Army, but I knew he wanted his only girl to have a civilian job where I could enjoy the stability of living and working in one place. Settle down. Marry. Have kids.

Dad suggested showing trust in my platoon sergeant, who was my second in command. "If you were injured or killed, he would be responsible for your soldiers in war," he said. "Show him that although you're the leader, you respect and trust his decisions. After all, a female giving orders is new to him. And above all, ask God for help."

Trust my platoon sergeant? Whenever I got in trouble with the commanding officer, he just stood by and watched. I was the one who got chewed out if things weren't right for inspection or if a soldier got in trouble downtown or a piece of equipment wasn't working. My platoon sergeant stood 6 feet to my 5-feet-5 inches. When I gave him an order, I had to look up into his hard gray eyes. He rarely spoke to me and spent all day with the soldiers. His desk was in their break room. When I gave him the soldiers' orders for the day, he said, "Yes ma'am," and walked away.

With his years in the military, his experience fighting in a war, and him being the age of my father—who was I to give him orders?

The next morning, after our daily run, I went to the shower room the soldiers and I shared. "Females Can't Lead" was scrawled on the shower wall. Furious, I had the platoon sergeant call the men together. I ordered them to do push-ups while I paced in front of them and shouted my reasons why I should lead. After their push-ups, while they stood exhausted and sweaty, I took away their weekend privileges and demanded they clean the shower wall.

I made a quick about-face and walked into the desert before they could see my tears. I remembered what my dad said about prayer. *Lord, help me learn how to be a good leader.*

After the soldiers went to work, I went to the platoon sergeant's office. He stood at attention when he saw me.

"At ease," I said. "I need your help. I have a lot to learn about leadership." He relaxed, and his eyes softened.

"First," he said, "you must know your soldiers." The next day, he gave me each soldier's personnel file. There I found out their hometowns and the names of their family members. Then he handed me their job descriptions. "Know what they do in the fire control van," he said.

While the soldiers were at lunch, I stood inside the van surrounded by dials, gauges, and red and yellow blinking lights. As a new officer attending the Air Defense Artillery School, I had listened as the instructor quickly covered the van's complex operation. But my soldiers had undergone months of extensive training. Leaving the control van, I took a manual home to study.

The next day, while the soldiers worked on the equipment inside the van, I looked over their shoulders. I asked to set one of the gauges. They were patient with me when I messed up the controls and they had to reset them.

During breaks, I asked soldiers about their families. At first they looked at me with suspicion. Then they'd start talking about *back home,* pulling out pictures of children, wives, and girlfriends.

One day, the platoon sergeant suggested we have a barbecue with the men on a Saturday. He offered to cook the meat. I gladly volunteered to bring the trimmings. I showed up in jeans, sneakers, and a T-shirt. No cap with a gold bar sat on my head. The men playfully teased me about how young I looked out of uniform. The platoon sergeant and I served up the food, and I surprised the men with a homemade chocolate cake.

Afterward, we played sand volleyball. We divided up the teams: the platoon sergeant versus the lieutenant. The final score was tied!

Later that evening, a brilliant sun lowered itself behind the cascading mountain range. My platoon sergeant and I sat outside the fire control van. We talked about our soldiers, our families, and why God allows wars to happen.

Two months before the missile launch, my platoon sergeant moved his desk into my office.

"The men must work harder on their drills to prepare them for the missile launch. They need to see you and me working together as a team," he said.

We practiced our drills late into the evenings and on the weekends. The soldiers showed me how to use the radar system to locate an enemy target and the missile's location as it soared through the air. The speed and accuracy of the information I reported to the first sergeant was critical to our mission.

The night before the launch, I walked into the desert where the Nike-Hercules missile sat waiting. *Thank you, Lord, for giving me a second chance with my soldiers.*

AFTER THE MISSILE launch, we headed back to headquarters to celebrate. Strolling behind my soldiers, I heard their tales of how their lieutenant didn't flinch under pressure when firing the missile. My platoon sergeant winked at me. I smiled.

Driving home from McGregor Range, a long, white streak lingered where the missile had traveled across the blue desert sky. My dad's advice to reach out to my soldiers, and their willingness to help me, caused our platoon to make history that day.

A time to break
down, and a time
to build up

TRANSFORMED OVER TIME

— By Debra Kornfield —

"**MOM, I RECOGNIZE** that building!" exclaimed five-year-old Rachel.

"That's because we've driven past it five or six times." I sighed. "I still don't know how to get home from here."

Nine-year-old Danny put his hand on my shoulder. "It's OK, Mommy. We're not really lost. Of all the cities in the world, we're in the right one!"

I still don't know how my four young children and I made it back to our apartment from my first venture grocery shopping by car in São Paulo, Brazil. I thought I knew the way, but amid traffic and street vendors and crowds of pedestrians and endless high rises, the streets looked alike to me. All the streets seemed to have three- or four-word names that jumbled in my mind along with our equally incomprehensible new address.

Why on earth didn't I write it down? Because I thought I knew it. My husband, Dave, was home and could have given it to me, but we didn't have a telephone.

I had also thought I understood the currency and how to think in kilos and grams instead of pounds and ounces. But by the time I selected bananas for 27,000 *cruzeiros novos* per kilo and a pineapple for 46,000 *cruzeiros novos* and mangos for 33,000 *cruzeiros novos* per kilo along with our other groceries, the zeros swirled in my head. My budding Portuguese wasn't adequate for whatever the cashier told me. When people in line behind me began to mutter, I dumped out the bills and coins I had with me, and the cashier picked through them to find what I owed.

Everything about São Paulo—20 million people crammed into impossibly small spaces—intimidated and confused me. Pedestrians had no rights; cars didn't stop when we tried to cross streets. On the standing-room-only buses, I feared a kidnapper would snatch one of my children for ransom, a frequent occurrence in our new city, especially for foreign children. Each time I arrived home safely after driving somewhere, I sat in the car trembling, saying, "Thank You, Lord, thank You, Lord, thank You, Lord," until He calmed me enough to move on to my next task.

Brazilians were lovely, hospitable, charming, and patient. Portuguese intrigued me. But the city terrified me. My childhood in a Mayan indigenous village in the highlands of Guatemala had given me no skills to survive in São Paulo.

"Lord, please," I prayed desperately, several times a day. "You guided us here. Please teach me to love this place. Show me how to feel at home here."

Yet city shock did not relent. Learning some missionary wives simply refused to drive in São Paulo comforted me only slightly. But my husband traveled, so I had to drive.

In the context of this insecurity, an email from Detroit shocked me to my core. I had written our daughter Karis's doctor for advice because she wasn't doing well.

"Dr. P. has retired," the email announced. "He is no longer available for consultation."

The words whirled. I had believed I trusted God with our chronically ill daughter's well-being in Brazil. In a flash, I realized that

> Because he bends
> down to listen, I will
> pray as long as
> I have breath!
> —Psalm 116:2 (NLT)
>
> ～

Dr. P. had been my security blanket. He had cared for Karis since she was two. He knew her "inside out" because of the surgeries he had performed on her. I counted on his guidance to manage Karis's rare condition: what diet might help, which medication to try. Twice in six months we had flown to Detroit for additional surgeries. Dr. P. never mentioned his plans to retire.

I wrote to Dr. P.'s partner. Surely, he would step in. But Dr. S. said no, he had no idea how to help Karis. "Find her a doctor in Brazil," he wrote me.

I tried. I asked everyone I knew for recommendations. For months, I crisscrossed our huge city, dragging Karis from one doctor's office to another. Their pronouncements were not encouraging.

"What you say she has doesn't exist. It's not a diagnosis. I can't accept a patient whose parent lies to me."

"You should just be thankful she's kept as well as she has for this long. Accept it; there's nothing to be done for her."

"Let's try this . . ." It turned out to be an excruciating procedure that didn't help.

"Feed her like this . . ." Her rapid weight loss only accelerated.

I yelled at God, tried to bargain with Him, or simply wept my helplessness in odd moments alone. Karis's teachers piled pillows in the back of her classroom so she could lie down when she needed to, thus staying in school more hours, more often. She had permission to run out of the classroom as necessary to throw up or manage her diarrhea. Loving teachers stopped by our home to help her with schoolwork when she was too sick to attend classes.

Meanwhile, my husband's ministry flourished. God did amazing things. Dave's enthusiasm for his work was boundless, leaving him little time to engage with his ill daughter and worried wife.

"Trust God!" he exhorted me. "Clearly, we're doing the right thing in the right place. Maybe this is a test of our faith or commitment."

Maybe it was. God felt as far away from me as my husband felt. I grew numb, going through the motions of my mission responsibilities and the care of my family. I knew the answers to other people's needs and questions. I could lead inspiring Bible studies for the women who looked to me for spiritual input. But as Karis grew worse, my heart deadened. I stopped trying to find a doctor for her. "This is on You, God."

Simple survival became my daily goal.

ON A MINI-FURLOUGH after 7 years in Brazil, I sat in a required meeting with our mission leaders, listening to Dave tell one glorious ministry story after another. Suddenly, a woman turned to me. "Tell us about you," she said. "How are you?"

Startled, I found myself saying, "I don't think I can go back to Brazil. I can't do this anymore. I can't."

"Do what?" she asked.

A dam broke, releasing my frustration, my fatigue, my fears. My husband sat with his mouth open while I wept over our children. Our son, whose gentleness had made him a target for bullies at school. Our Rachel, who buried herself in books, preferring fantasies to the reality of our home. Our youngest, Valerie, once a bright ray of sunshine, had become a shadow of herself. And Karis, who was bravely fighting, but losing, the battle for her life. I wept over my inadequacy to care for them while carrying the ministry burdens my husband expected me to manage.

Inside, even while responding to the group's insightful questions, I berated myself. *What a wimp! Look at the kind of missionary you are!*

Instead of supporting your husband's ministry, you'll become known for sabotaging it. Stop this! Apologize! Minimize! Get your act together!

But our mission leaders didn't echo that critical voice. They did not shame me. They listened. They conferred, not about disciplining their disappointing missionary, but about how to care for me. The idea that *I* needed care took a while to penetrate my defenses.

In the end, we returned to Brazil, but I was placed on sabbatical, first for 6 months, then 12, then 18. All I was "allowed" to do was care for myself and my family. Dave learned to function without me as his right arm. A counselor taught me healthy boundaries, margins, and appropriate self-care.

Shortly after we returned to Brazil, we received another gift: an amazing doctor for Karis. Dr. G. practiced medicine not just as science, but also as art. We loved and trusted him, literally, with Karis's life. He taught me faith isn't as simple as either blind trust in God alone or an unhealthy dependence on human wisdom. Instead, during that time in Brazil, God cared for us *through* the people and resources He placed in our lives: A doctor who understood both Karis's syndrome and her bright mind and her dreams. A mission team that cared for and supported and taught me. A school whose teachers guided Karis to the honors program at Notre Dame. A Brazilian church that loved us.

That was 25 years ago. Last week, my daughter Rachel, now a mother herself, said, "Mom, do you know what I remember as the best time of my childhood? Those months you were on sabbatical. Our house felt like a home, not a ministry center. I'm grateful to our mission leaders for their wisdom."

Those years in Brazil were a time to break down and a time to build up: a time to tear down pride and self-sufficiency and unmanageable stress—and a time to repair and restore bruised hearts and heal frayed relationships, as the Lord bent to care for our needs.

TO EAT OR NOT TO EAT

— By Amy Wallace —

WHAT DOES FOOD mean to you? For me, food has always represented great comfort. Birthday cakes celebrate another year of life; turkey and pumpkin pie prompt thankfulness; and Christmas cookies warm cold nights and lonely days. Curling up with a good book and a cup of cocoa or a movie and a bucket of popcorn means escape and laughter and safety.

While food means celebration and comfort to me, and culture, church, and copious TV ads echo that idea, food can also lead to a deep, dark pit.

My first foray into the pit of an eating disorder started after a serious illness left me with chronic pain and no energy. At the end of a painful day, I'd collapse on my couch, click the remote, and lose myself in TV and treats. For a time, that escape numbed the pain.

What began as a once-a-month indulgence became every week, then every day. What started as a few cookies became eating until I felt sick, even when I didn't want the first bite.

One evening, I sat in front of the TV with a bag of chips, intending to eat only a few. Once that bag was gone, I made trip after trip back to the kitchen, and box after box of crackers and containers of mixed nuts disappeared. I watched another show and the buzz of numbness faded, so I made another trip to the kitchen. I was so desperate that I started eating raw sugar.

I was sick for days, so full I could barely move, so ashamed that I couldn't look my children in the eyes, and I hid from friends.

God broke through my shame daze with an online Bible study a friend invited me to read with her. As I pored over the daily devotions about the author's struggle with food, I saw myself in every word. I sat in my bed at night and took notes: *I know with my head that God alone satisfies, but my heart is quick to run after easy, and food is easy satisfaction. I want food more than I want God.* As I wrote in my journal each night, I began to understand that my comfort eating was not only an eating disorder but also an idol. One that had to fall before I destroyed myself.

I saw that I ran to food more than to God. I trusted food more than God to comfort me.

That realization dropped me to my knees. I prayed and confessed and quoted Scripture and walked away from binge eating for a day, then a week, then a month, then a total of 101 days. Food controlled me no longer.

Except it did. On my one hundred and second day of no snacking, no eating at night, no going over my calorie limit, I broke. Nothing set me off, no bad news or worsening pain. I just wanted to eat, and so I did. I thought about praying, but I ignored the Holy Spirit's warning in my heart and walked right into the kitchen. I picked up a container of nuts, and then crackers, and I ate for hours. I cried as I ate. I tried to pray, but I kept running to the fridge instead to quiet the guilt and shame echoing in my thoughts. I'd tried my best and done everything I knew to do, and I'd failed. I would never be free of this eating disorder.

I gave up praying and trying and all the rules I'd read about in devotions, online articles, and books about eating disorders, all the rules that were supposed to help me but didn't. I talked to no one about this idol that now controlled every waking thought and kept me going through the day to get to the place where I could eat in private.

Then I noticed my kids had started staying up later and asking for some of my chips or crackers or nuts. What started as joining me for a treat once a week became every night, and I started to see the same anguish in their eyes that I ignored in my mirror.

Food had captured my kids.

Like stepping into the sun from a dark cave, the haze cleared, and I saw my children mindlessly eating. I saw them following me down a dangerous path, and I finally understood that there was no secret sin, no way to hide an idol forever, and no way to heal from an eating disorder alone. What I wouldn't do for me, I had to do for my kids. I had only joked with a few friends about struggling with food. I had never told anyone just how bad my eating disorder had become, how much I loved food more than God. I was too ashamed, too protective of my idol to let the truth come out.

I wouldn't let my kids go down this same path. I prayed a desperate prayer and scoured my church's website, looking for someone who could help me. I found an email for a stranger at church who led a women's group for eating disorders. I reached out to her and poured out my saga, every ugly detail. I told her what I knew to be true about food idolatry, what I'd tried to do to save myself, how my food disorder was hurting my kids, and how I was hopeless and helpless.

I expected to feel shame. I expected to be judged and told

> So whether you eat or drink, or whatever you do, do it all for the glory of God.
> —1 Corinthians 10:31 (NLT)

better ways to try harder and pray more. What I received was a gift of God in the form of a Bible study I didn't want and a friend I had no idea how much I needed.

My new friend thanked me for sharing my story and told me I was brave. She also told me there was hope. Over email first and then in person, she shared with me about her struggle with an eating disorder and how God had become real to her in the midst of her pain. I could hear in her words and see in her gentleness and focus on prayer that she loved the Lord, and the Lord had worked powerfully in her life. We started meeting every week for months to work through the most honest and idol-breaking Bible study I'd ever seen. The study, *The Woman in the Mirror*, was written by a gracious lady who also battled an eating disorder, and rather than being given a list of dos and don'ts, I was invited into God's Word to see God's greatness, His love for me, and His power over idols.

God's timing was so perfect. Just as I reached the end of my ability to cope and my heart was desperate enough to change, He sent this Bible study and this friend to walk through it with me and show me I wasn't alone. Only then was I able to receive and grow so much.

I learned to listen to the lies I told myself and replace them with truth. I learned that I did care about my body and that I needed to take care of it to honor God. I learned that there was hope.

I learned that I had a choice: to eat or not to eat. To sin and run to food or to run to God. To think about food or think about my Savior.

I also learned that failure was part of the process.

I wish I could say that I've never been tempted to binge, never started down that path after finishing the Bible study. I can't. What I can say is that I've prayed through the holidays and devastating news and health crises that have come, and there have been more moments of victory, more time spent with God, and more reaching out to others to give and receive help.

I'm no longer in this battle alone, and neither are my kids. We have a God who loves us, a church family who cares for us, and friends who not only know about but also join in the fight with us.

There is now hope.

To eat or not to eat is no longer the question. My focus now is on the question, How do I love Jesus and allow Him to love me today? That question has a beautiful answer: taste and see that the Lord is good. Indeed, He is.

CHAPTER
3

MOVING BEYOND GRIEF

ECCLESIASTES 3:4

A time to weep,
and a time to laugh;
a time to mourn,
and a time to dance

INTRODUCTION

Stories of mourning and the laughter and dancing that helped them through it

— By Shirley Raye Redmond —

COULD SHE DANCE? Not a chance.

Run? Most unlikely.

Born premature and weighing less than 5 pounds, African American Wilma Rudolph (1940–1994) was crippled with polio in her infancy. Doctors told her mother that Wilma would never walk properly. Wilma was nearly two years old before she began toddling around the house, forced to wear a heavy brace on her left leg. No one predicted that one day Wilma Glodean Rudolph from Tennessee would become one of the fastest female runners in the world. That she would one day win three Olympic gold medals was unimaginable.

Undaunted by her child's disability, Blanche Rudolph, Wilma's determined mother, firmly believed that God could and would heal her young daughter. She took Wilma to church every Sunday and held family devotions each evening. When doctors recommended physical therapy for Wilma, Blanche dutifully drove her daughter to the hospital—100 miles round trip—to keep each appointment.

Wilma longed to rip and run with her 21 siblings, so her brothers put up a basketball hoop and taught an eager Wilma how to play. By the time Wilma was 12 years old, she no longer needed the leg brace. She kept exercising and practiced running short distances. As she grew stronger, she joined the high school track team, where she was spotted by a coach for Tennessee State University, who invited her to join his summer training program. She began going to track meets—and winning.

In 1956, at the age of 16, Wilma traveled to Melbourne, Australia, with the US Olympic track and field team. There she won a bronze medal for the 400-meter relay, and her strikingly graceful running style gained her many fans among the spectators and journalists. In 1960, Wilma was in top physical condition for the Olympics in Rome. She didn't ask God to let her win her races. She prayed only that He would help her do her best. Wilma raced with amazing speed, becoming the first woman to ever win three track-and-field gold medals in one Olympic year.

Because the games were broadcast on television in North America for the very first time, Wilma became an overnight sensation. When officials back home in Clarksville, Tennessee, offered to hold a segregated celebration in her honor, Wilma politely refused to attend unless everyone could be in the same space. The welcome home parade and banquet that followed were the first integrated social events in Clarksville.

The apostle Paul compared Christian discipleship to the training and self-sacrifice of a dedicated athlete. Wilma Rudolph's life is a good illustration of the sort of discipline and dedication one needs to live a fulfilling Christian life in which hardship and self-sacrifice are blessed with joy and laughter.

IN THE CHAPTER that follows, you will find stories that might remind you of Wilma's struggle and ultimate victory: A woman whose left arm is paralyzed from childhood polio finds new confidence in a chance gift. Another woman mourning the loss of a child who finds solace in running. People who experience unexpected laughter in moments of sadness; people who find little ways to come back to life after a loss. Along each step, we're reminded how all things are made new when God is near.

I GOT RHYTHM

— By Louis Lotz —

WHEN I WAS a boy—14 years old, 15 maybe—a great ice storm blew in from the Atlantic and swept across the eastern seaboard, from Delaware to Maine, toppling power lines and knocking down thousands of trees, one of which was in our backyard. It was a towering maple with a trunk as thick as a trash can. The next morning, my father and I trooped out to the backyard to saw up the downed tree with a two-man saw.

You see two-man saws in old black-and-white photos of turn-of-the-century lumberjacks and logging camps. The saw had a toothy metal blade about 4 feet long, and there was a wood handle at each end. Nowadays, nobody uses two-man saws. The only place you'll find them is in an antique shop. But in the right hands, a two-man saw is a formidable tool, and it can make quick work of even the thickest trees.

My father loved that saw. I can remember him oiling the blade and sharpening it with a file, putting a knife edge on each tooth. When I timidly suggested one day that we ought to get a chain saw, he looked at me with disdain. "Folks who use chain saws are just afraid of hard work," he muttered. My father loved hard work. The harder, the better. He had sinewy, muscled forearms, and large, gnarly hands that looked like they could pry the lid off a rusted tar bucket.

But there is a certain rhythm, a give and take, that needs to exist between the two sawyers. Predictably, my father and I, who were not in sync on much of anything else in life, did not make good partners on the two-man saw. Looking back, I'm sure the fault was mostly mine. I pushed when I should have pulled. I held tight when I should have let loose. The long, gray blade bent and buckled and repeatedly hopped out of the groove. And all the while I could see my father getting angrier and angrier—at the storm, at the saw, at the tree, at me.

Finally, we stopped. My father sat down on the fallen tree. He lit his pipe and smoked in silence for a moment. Then, much to my surprise, he looked up at me with a big grin and said: "Son, there's a rhythm to this, and we ain't got it!" And he threw back his head and laughed. Then I began to laugh. We just sat there, the two of us, laughing uproariously, tears in our eyes. He started singing the Gershwin song "I Got Rhythm," which triggered another round of loud laughter.

Eventually, he slid his strong, muscled arm around my shoulder and hugged me. I was about to say something, but I was afraid I'd break the spell, so I just sat there in silence, leaning my head against his shoulder. In my whole life, I don't know if I ever felt closer to my father than I did in that moment. A week later, he went out and purchased a chain saw.

"For every thing there is a season," says Ecclesiastes. There is a rhythm to life, like the rhythm of a two-man saw. Give and take, come and go, push and pull. When you go against that rhythm, life seems to bend and buckle and you're not in the groove. I learned the hard way (which is pretty much how I learn everything) that when you keep trying to make something happen that clearly doesn't want to happen, it's not necessarily that you are doing something wrong. It's that the season changed, the rhythm shifted,

> So we have known and believe the love that God has for us. God is love, and those who abide in love abide in God, and God abides in them.
>
> −1 John 4:16 (NRSVUE)

~

and you didn't notice. You're pulling when it's time to push. You're holding tight when it's time to let loose.

But now and then, by God's grace, we get it right. My father didn't throw away the two-man saw—heaven forbid—but he somehow sensed that it was time to purchase a chain saw. I think we both learned something, he and me, on that magic day, sitting on the fallen log, the sweet smell of pipe smoke in the air.

Fast-forward 30 years. The kindly police officer on the telephone said that although my father's car was parked out front, he didn't answer the door, didn't answer the phone. The neighbors were getting worried. A locksmith was summoned, and he opened the front door and cut the security chain with a bolt cutter. They found my father lying crossways on the bed. He was 78.

A week later, my sister and I met at his condo to go through his personal belongings. As we were rummaging through a closet, my sister found a phonograph and a stack of old 78 rpm records, each stored in a brown paper sleeve. The third record from the top of the pile was Gershwin's "I Got Rhythm."

A time to
weep, and a
time to laugh

SHINY RED PLASTIC

— By Linda S. Clare —

I SAT ON the edge of the orthopedic exam table, nervously swinging my legs. The surgeon got right to the point. "You need a total shoulder replacement."

My eyes must have widened. I croaked, "Total? Can't I just do physical therapy?"

The doctor peered over his glasses "Your right shoulder's in rough shape. A total shoulder replacement is your only option." He frowned. "You'll need 6 weeks in the sling to recover."

"Six weeks?" I froze. The restrictive sling would pin my right arm to my waist. My left arm had limited mobility, and recovery without a backup arm sounded downright terrifying. One arm minus one arm equaled no arms. How would I live without arms for 6 long weeks?

"You don't understand." Panic scrabbled at my senses. I'm not a crier, but tears stung my lashes.

But the surgeon was matter of fact. "I understand that you'll need quite a bit of support during recovery. Visit an occupational therapist for some coping ideas. You'll be fine." The doc called for his surgery scheduler and left the room, his white coat flapping.

I sat there, stunned. *Why me? Why now?*

The first question I asked the therapist was how I could manage without my one good arm. I told her all about my life doing everything single-handedly after a childhood bout with polio had paralyzed my left arm and hand.

When I was nine, my dad had watched as I tried to will my left hand to turn a doorknob. No dice. "Ask God for a way," Dad said. "God's always on time." Ashamed at my lack of faith, I'd turned away so Dad wouldn't see me cry.

To cope, I decided to laugh at myself instead of crying. I became a miniature comedian. I poked fun at myself as I figured out ways to learn to swim and ride a bike. "Ha ha," I'd tell my friends. "Look, Ma, one hand!" For every challenge I faced, I compensated by cracking jokes or acting as if I didn't care.

Secretly, though, I *did* care. As I hit my teens, I became self-conscious, hiding my paralysis whenever I could. I still kept up my comedy routine, but instead of flaunting my lack of mobility, I carefully disguised it. After all, I needed acceptance, especially by the opposite sex. Guys said I was smart, fairly good-looking, and funny. Really funny. Trouble was, I wasn't sure if they meant funny *ha ha* or funny as in *strange*. At night, I wept quietly into my pillow and begged God to show me the way.

I met a good man, got married, and started a family. When God gave me surprise twins, I made jokes about the divine logic of giving two babies to one-handed me. And whenever tasks became as challenging as that sticky doorknob, I'd ask God to find a way.

By middle age, my "good" arm wasn't so good. I'd schlepped babies and car seats, assembled cribs and sewed clothes for my kids. Too much heavy lifting and wear and tear on my right arm left me with severe arthritis. I couldn't avoid the upcoming surgery.

I poured out my fears to the occupational therapist. "How will I take care of myself?" Brush my own hair? Pull up my pants?

Hook a brassiere? I pictured diving face-first into my dinner like I was in a pie-eating contest. Toileting needs? Suddenly, I was all out of humor. A tear slipped down my cheek.

Most of the aids the therapist offered were only helpful if you had at least one good hand to use—long-handled grabbers or special forks and spoons with exaggerated grips. Yet I saw little that might be useful to a no-handed person.

If you falter in a time of trouble, how small is your strength!

—Proverbs 24:10 (NIV)

Then the therapist demonstrated an extra-extra-long drinking straw. Suddenly, an idea hit me. "I love Diet Dr. Pepper," I told her. "It's my one bad habit," I kidded. "But I'm afraid I won't be able to twist open a bottle cap."

The therapist smiled and held up a piece of shiny red plastic about the size of a dollar bill. "This will open any jar or bottle," she said. "It's magical."

I cracked a joke. "I have a jar opener already. His name is Brad."

But the therapist insisted. At home, I tossed the shiny red plastic and giant drinking straw into my junk drawer and forgot it.

I survived my total shoulder replacement. Recovering at home, I learned to hate the sling as much as anyone in that situation would. The entire experience was one huge pain in the patootie.

Then one day, my husband was at work, and I was alone in the house. At first, I savored the quiet. I managed to make popcorn for an afternoon snack—who knew you could push the microwave's buttons with your nose? Then I poked my fingers out of the sling to grab a fresh bottle of Diet Dr. Pepper.

But the cap wouldn't budge. The harder I twisted, the more a searing pain shot through my arm and into my shoulder. I knew better than to bear down harder—the surgeon had warned me not to stress my arm.

With salty popcorn drying my mouth, I felt helpless. Like the doorknob that had beaten me as a nine-year-old, this bottle of soda pop seemed to mock me. I wanted to knock that bottle into next week. Tears again threatened.

Brad wouldn't be home for an hour. Yet my father's words floated back. *"Ask God for a way. He's always on time."* As I prayed, I thought of that shiny red plastic.

Suddenly, it hit me. For years I'd relied on my right arm's strength to get things done. But when I thought I was leaning on God, I'd foolishly relied on myself. I stood in awe of God's wisdom. He had brought to mind that silly piece of shiny red plastic at the perfect time, with the perfect answer to my prayer. It wasn't about a soda cap or an arm; it was about the ways that God was always there for me.

Still skeptical—of the therapist's contraption, but not of God's leading—I found the red plastic, positioned it over the soda's cap, and twisted gently. The bubbly *whoosh* told me that God's timing *is* perfect. I had to laugh—even without arms, God showed me a way.

SIDE BY SIDE

— By Jill Baughan —

YEARS AGO, MY mom and I were at the Virginia State Fair when we walked by a booth where you could get an Instamatic photo taken with a chimpanzee for a mere 5 dollars.

The very idea made me laugh, and, excited, I begged, "Hey Mom! Let's get our picture taken with the chimp! Please!"

But my mother, always more reserved than I was, repeatedly declined to participate in what I deemed the "opportunity of a lifetime." Finally, exasperated, I asked, "Why not?"

She thought for a minute and said, deadpan, "Well . . . someone might look at it 50 years from now and think it's a three-generation photo."

I had to admit, that was hard to dispute.

And, to my profound disappointment, we walked away, unphotographed. But I never forgot that lost opportunity.

FAST-FORWARD ABOUT 20 years. My husband and I were making preparations for a big event, and my family was coming to Virginia from Indiana to attend. One night, lying in bed, I was trying to think of a few meaningful activities for us to do together during their visit, and I had an idea: I had always regretted that lost opportunity

> You turned my wailing into dancing; you removed my sackcloth and clothed me with joy, that my heart may sing your praises and not be silent.
> —Psalm 30:11-12 (NIV)

~

at the state fair years before. Why not redeem it by finding a rentable, photogenic chimp and surprising my mom with an offer too good to refuse: a second chance to get our picture taken with a really cute primate?

I put out an all-points bulletin to everyone I knew, and eventually found a local gentleman who operated a zoo on his property and had a chimp who lived in his house. When I explained my plan to him, he said, "Oh sure, you can borrow Tootsie for a while. But it's December. You don't want your elderly mother out in the cold. Why don't I bring her to your house?"

Perfect! And 2 weeks later, once my family had arrived, I gave him a thumbs-up call. When I saw him come up the walk with Tootsie, I put my arm around my mom and said, "Put some lipstick on, Mom. I've got a surprise for you."

When the door opened and she saw the chimp, she knew exactly what I was up to, and this time—having mellowed out a bit between ages 68 and 88—she was very excited for a second chance at some fun. And fun we had. I had arranged for a photographer to come and record the historic occasion, and for the next 90 minutes, we frolicked with that chimp like we had never frolicked before. She jumped all over us, turned somersaults with us, took grapes from our mouths, rolled over us as we lay on the floor, and in general acted like the two-year-old she was. Three hundred photos later, we were exhausted. Honestly, I had never seen my mom laugh so much or so hard.

It was one of those days that are beyond memorable, with too many precious moments to count. We even had a family portrait taken with Tootsie in front, like she was one of the cousins. After that, the moment of redemption came when Mom and I posed for our long-delayed picture with a chimpanzee. But honestly, the very best part of the day was when Tootsie and Mom sat down to have their photo taken together.

Well, "sat down" was not entirely accurate. Tootsie was all over my mom, jumping into her lap, bumping noses, and bouncing around her like the 88-year-old was her very own mother.

Finally we got Tootsie to settle down a bit by bribing her with a couple of grapes, and the photographer snapped a priceless side-by-side shot of my mom with her arm around the little ape, both of them facing the camera, and both (yes, *both*) doing a show-your-teeth smile.

I framed that picture and put it on my dresser, where it still sits, and never stopped thanking God for that day. It became the stuff of family legends.

ELEVEN YEARS LATER, my mom passed away at age 99. She had lived a long, amazing life, but saying goodbye is never easy. Even when you know it's "time," even when you know your loved one is ready for heaven, sorrow prevails.

My brother and I wanted her celebration of life service to reflect the joy that she brought to the world. We certainly didn't want to deny the presence of grief; there was plenty of that. But we wanted to create space for celebration to synchronize with that grief.

So as we began our plans, we prayed for a way to honor our mother with joy through our tears. We prayed that, as we remembered her, there would be many smiles and much laughter, that the stories we told would remind us all just how fortunate we were to have known her, and that God would fill the atmosphere with energy and show us just how much fun He can be.

I know, rather unusual requests for a funeral. But may I just say that God doesn't mess around when you pray for inspiration like that?

He answered those prayers in a most unexpected way, leading us to choose absolutely buoyant prelude music that included a collection of songs from the playlist of the Greatest Generation. Because, we reasoned, who can resist smiling when, mixed in with great music like "His Eye Is on the Sparrow" and "How Great Thou Art," you're listening to "In the Mood," "Chattanooga Choo Choo," "Stompin' at the Savoy," and "Side by Side"?

When the funeral director told us they needed a photo for the memorial pamphlet to offer folks at the visitation, we thought about it for a minute. Then my brother said quietly, "I have an idea, but it might be inappropriate."

I knew exactly what he was thinking and said, "Are you kidding? There could be no better photo than that one!"

So the image that greeted friends and family who came to remember Mary was a playful picture of her, smiling, with her arm around a chimpanzee. We had such a good time telling everyone the story behind the photo.

And because of this story and others, because of the uplifting music (which actually elicited enthusiastic applause), and because of our hope in the God of all comfort, we were able to ask our broken hearts to move over and make room for celebration to walk alongside our sorrow. In fact, two people at the service stopped the director and said they wanted to meet with him to change a few prearranged plans they'd made for their own funerals. They wanted to include more joy, they said.

Because God—as God is so prone to do when life takes a heavy hearted turn—showed us how to make sure that joy arrived just in time, at just the right moment for us all.

THE LINGERING SCENT OF MY MOTHER'S PERFUME

— By Lynne Hartke —

I BLAMED MY memory lapse on too much sugar.

As in sugar cookies, gingerbread men, cinnamon rolls, and fudge. All the Christmas sugary goodness.

Usually, I stripped my office of all interesting knickknacks when the grandchildren came over, leaving only books and framed photos on the shelves. This time, as I settled my four-year-old grandson, Micah, down for a nap, I thought, *He's only in the room for 1 hour, and he'll be sleeping. How much trouble can one little boy get into?* Decades of parenting and grandparenting wisdom evaporated in my sugary delirium.

"The room smells nice," I said to Micah at the end of naptime. I gazed around the room for the source of the scent. "Did you put lotion on your hands?"

"No," Micah said. His voice dropped to a conspiratorial whisper. "Magic potion."

"Magic potion?" I asked in my no-nonsense teacher voice. "Where did you find magic potion?"

Micah scampered off the bed. He picked up a sample-sized bottle of perfume on the floor, perfume I thought—until that moment—had been safely stored on a high shelf above my desk.

The shelf held a few things that had belonged to my mother, Micah's great-grandmother.

Mom had died almost 2 years earlier from cancer, just 9 months after Dad. The stinging pain of grief had passed, but the second year contained the finality of it all. In the silent weight of loss, I had struggled to find Christmas in the decorating. In the shopping. In the baking. The present celebration without Mom and Dad had threatened to overwhelm me. Since I wasn't sure if the Christmas spirit would find me this year, I had kept moving. But that is all it had been—going through the motions.

I straightened the office shelf Micah had jiggled, noticing the empty spot for the bottle of perfume. It mirrored the emptiness my heart still experienced, especially for my mom. I missed Mom's role as the family's biggest cheerleader. I missed her voice on the other end of the phone. I missed her scent.

"God, please fill up the missing," I whispered, feeling the familiar ache.

Mom had worn a famous scent, advertised to contain the fragrance of a thousand flowers, with notes of roses, lilies, marigolds, and sandalwood, that offered a pleasing invitation and lasting impression. Mom had lived up to the scent's description in aroma and in character. Her kindness, faith, and trust in God lingered like a garden bouquet whenever she had entered the room.

Like a time machine, the familiar scent transported me back to the final Christmas we had spent together at the family farm in Minnesota, our extended family drawn together by the news that both our parents had been diagnosed with stage-four cancer.

TWENTY OF US had traveled from California, Texas, Arizona, Colorado, and other parts of the United States with borrowed boots and winter coats, via airplanes and rental cars, until we had pulled into the driveway of Mom and Dad's country acreage. We had stumbled on too-stiff legs toward the waiting silhouettes under the porch light and held on tight, words spilling, *did-you-have-a-good-trip, it's-good-to-see-you, look-how-tall-you-have-grown.*

> **Pleasing is the fragrance of your perfumes; your name is like perfume poured out.**
> **—Song of Songs 1:3 (NIV)**
>
> ❧

Getting into the kitchen involved a receiving line of shoulder-slapping, neck-hugging relatives with Mom asking, "Do you want something to eat?" Food overflowed in the dining room, where we grabbed chairs and slid out a second table stored behind the couch. Dad said grace as we held hands in a room-for-one-more circle with bowed heads and lumps in our throats.

Finally, we passed out in exhaustion on beds wherever we could find them, but our grown children—the cousins—had stayed awake in the basement later than all of us, playing games while huddled around the space heater. Up through the vents in the floor laughter drifted, while snow and icy rain fell outside.

After breakfast, Mom had rolled out *kringla*—a Scandinavian bow-shaped cookie—and *lefse*—a Norwegian flatbread—promising samples to her helpers.

"The first ones out of the oven feed the cook!" Mom declared—like she always did—passing the flour-covered memories to eager fingers.

Amid conversations of weddings and babies, school plans and jobs, chemo treatments and the possibility of selling the farm, Dad had entered the house smelling like his Allis-Chalmers tractor. He had plowed the long driveway, clearing a path in the fresh-fallen snow.

Chaos arrived with the grandchildren, bundled in winter layers for a slide down the small hill on the back property, something my siblings and I had enjoyed at their age. The smell of fresh air and winter skies melted down their reddened cheeks.

"Who wants hot chocolate?" Mom asked as she grabbed candy canes from the pantry for stirring sticks, her query met with resounding cheers.

I COULD ALMOST smell the peppermint as Micah tugged me back to the present when he handed me the small vial of Mom's perfume. "Here," he said, his face still filled with wonder. "Magic potion."

Checking the bottle, I was relieved to notice only a small amount of the perfume had spilled, although *spilled* was not an accurate term. *Transferred* would have been closer to the truth.

Transferred to my grandson's hands. His arms. His shirt. The bedding.

"You smell like Great-Grandma," his mother said a few minutes later, having been informed of his naptime misdemeanors. Micah nodded and ran off to play with trucks and building blocks, a young boy, full of energy, smelling like my mother.

And just like that, Christmas found me, with the lingering scents of yesterday perfuming my current reality. The missing places inside me filled with hope and promise as I made a decision to create memories for my children and grandchildren, like my mom had done before me.

I returned to my office to put the perfume safely away in a drawer. The name on the bottle caught my eye: *Beautiful* by Estee Lauder. I smiled.

The perfume lived up to its name in a way the manufacturers could never have imagined. The original wearer of the scent was no longer with us, but the next generation, while running around in puppy-dog underwear, spread the aroma of memory throughout the house. He opened my mind to understand something he had already recognized. Sometimes magic is hiding right in front of our eyes.

Or under our noses.

A time to
mourn, and a
time to dance

THE ORANGE TREE

— By Leslie McLeod —

THE SPRAWLING ORANGE tree in our California backyard
had long been a source of nourishment, comfort, and fun. Our
children and their friends had played hide-and-seek among its
leafy branches, enjoyed picnics under its shade, plucked its round
fruit for an impromptu ball game. The tree cheerfully shared of its
juicy, seedless abundance with our family, friends, and thirsty youth
soccer players. My friend Janice and I inhaled the sweet fragrance as
we watched our girls dance and decorate each other's hair with its
blossoms.

Over time, the children grew into young adults, and I found
myself entering a season of seismic life shifts. Empty nest. Aging
parents. Hormonal changes. Janice, who had since moved away with
her daughter, was diagnosed with cancer.

The orange tree, which had remained lush and productive,
began to show signs of distress. Some leaves curled and turned black
along the edges. Insects boldly took up residence, and the tree was
unable to fend off their advances. Impotent in the face of looming
loss on so many other fronts, I poured my energy into caring for
the tree. I researched possible diseases, looking for treatments that
wouldn't harm the fruit. I tried sprays, physical barriers around the
trunk, selective pruning to encourage the healthy branches. Still it

continued to struggle, while I continued to obsess. The other trees in our backyard were fine—why was our favorite suffering?

"God, will You save my tree?" I prayed. I begged. Bartered. Tried to reason with Him. "It's been such a lovely tree for so many years. Countless people have been blessed by its fruit. I don't care about the other orange tree—it has a ton of seeds. Let that one get sick instead. Just rescue this one, please. I know You can."

I laid hands on the ailing citrus, proclaiming, "Be healed, O Orange Tree," adding, "in Jesus's name," for good measure.

Nothing happened.

Now, I'm not prone to hearing the voice of God, audibly or otherwise. But a short time later, while I was walking my elderly dog, I sensed this distinct message: *I'm teaching you to say goodbye, gently.*

I understood that, in His kindness, He was preparing me to let go.

"Okay," I responded humbly. "But can't You do that without killing my tree?"

It was summertime, and our family had planned one last vacation before our son and daughter moved out to attend college. We had a wonderful trip. On our return, I rushed to the backyard to see how the orange tree was faring.

I burst into tears.

Nearly all the tree's leaves were withered and yellow. Many had fallen to the ground, and the branches were naked of fruit or flowers. Hoping that perhaps I had misheard God's words, I made an appointment with a professional arborist to come and assess the tree's condition.

The uniformed tree man came to our front door and asked where the patient was. I gestured out the sliding glass door beyond our dining room.

"Why, there's nothing wrong with that tree," he pronounced. "It looks perfectly healthy!"

> Peace I leave with you; my peace I give you. I do not give to you as the world gives. Do not let your hearts be troubled and do not be afraid.
> —John 14:27 (NIV)

"Not that one," I said, frowning. "Look over there to the left."

His gaze followed mine to the pathetic-looking specimen just beyond his immediate line of sight.

"Oh, that one's history," the arborist declared.

We ventured outside so he could take a closer look. On inspection, he explained that the beautiful tree we'd enjoyed for decades had been originally grafted onto a fast-growing, weed-like root when it was part of the commercial grove that once occupied our property. The root had continued to grow at a disproportionate rate, eventually choking out the healthy tree from within.

"So there's nothing I could have done to save it?" I asked.

"Afraid not," he said, scratching his head. "It was just a matter of time."

I thanked him, strangely relieved. I had tried everything, but the outcome was—and had always been—out of my hands. His prognosis confirmed God's message to my heart.

Over the next weeks, I refused help as I took on the project of cutting down the orange tree myself, branch by branch. The tree seemed unwilling to give up without a fight. Previously unseen thorns pricked my hands. I almost fell off the ladder more than once. It was by God's grace that I didn't accidentally remove one of my own limbs with the heavy rented power saw.

The hard physical work gave time and substance to my grief as I cried and cursed and slowly let go. Through the arduous process, I came to terms with the fact that I cannot hold off inevitable change: the pain of loss. What God allowed, I could somehow face.

During this time, I was deeply saddened to receive word that Janice was in the last stages of her battle with cancer—that I would soon have to let go of my dear friend. In and out of a coma, she seemed restless, unsettled in her spirit. I knew as a single mom she was anxious about leaving her 20-year-old daughter. But the young woman was ready, and she assured her mother that she would be okay. Still Janice hung on, seemingly unable to let go.

The orange tree seemed to symbolize my friend's journey in a way that I thought she might relate to. A picture of vitality and strength, of illness and resistance, of submission and release. So I wrote her its simple story, reminding her of God's intimate presence, His beautiful purpose for her earthly life, now fulfilled. *Trust Him,* I said. *He holds you now as He always has.* I emailed it to her family, who read it to her that evening, unsure if she was even able to hear the words.

The next morning, my friend slipped away peacefully.

When my children moved out that fall and my season of loss flowed along its natural course, my heart ached, but I was no longer afraid. He had taught me to say goodbye.

Gently.

A time to
mourn, and a
time to dance

A TIME FOR DANCING

— By Cindy Shufflebarger —

DESPITE BEING A shy, insecure teen, I had loved the allure of attending dances in junior high school. While the events were always a huge step out of my comfort zone, they enticed me, offering the hope that a cute boy would ask me to dance or that I could dance uninhibited, surrounded by a multitude of friends and the fun of the music. However, the evening was often different from what I imagined, ranging from disappointment that I wasn't asked to dance to panic when the wrong guy invited me onto the dance floor. I was too self-conscious to truly enjoy dancing. But, oh, how I longed for the freedom to dance without a care.

Years later, I was engaged to marry a man with no rhythm. When we were dating, Scott and I attempted line dancing. His size-12 boots could be better described as weapons. I was left with bruised shins and at least one bloody toe. The instructor called right and he went left—right into me—a few too many times.

My dream of dancing dimmed a little more. But we held out hope. Surely we could learn to waltz in time to enjoy our first dance at our wedding. No boots were involved, so I hoped that all skin would remain intact.

We lived in a small town, so dance opportunities were limited, but we managed to find a ballroom dance club. Surely they'd welcome some youthful souls. About halfway through the first night, the male instructor broke in and led me to another area of the dance floor while the female instructor grabbed my soon-to-be husband.

An hour later we reconvened in the middle of the room and the woman apologized, insisting that she'd done her best, but it appeared a hopeless cause. They suggested we find something else to do. My dream of dancing was dashed one final time.

Life got busy. We had careers, then kids and new pursuits. Time marched on. We didn't really have opportunities to dance anyway, so my desire to dance was forgotten.

As my oldest daughter entered her teens, I insisted that she participate in some sort of physical activity and a musical endeavor. She wasn't into sports and no longer played a musical instrument, but when I discovered a ballroom dance group for teens, she grudgingly agreed to attend.

At first, she hated it. As the year progressed, however, she began to enjoy dancing and discovered she was good at it. She participated in ballroom dance for 6 more years, becoming a member of the leadership team, exhibition team, and an instructor. Along the way, she recruited Scott to be one of the designated adult dancers (DADs) because they always needed extra guys to even the ratio of males to females. And so, slowly, my husband learned to dance.

I was shocked. The directors of the program were encouraging and patient . . . and then patient some more. After 8 years of dancing with his daughters, he finally got the hang of it. He still struggled to hear the beat sometimes, but he was proficient enough to enjoy it.

Along the way, as our other children were old enough, they began dancing, too—by choice. There have also been adult classes offered so that I was able to learn to dance with Scott, and now we all can dance. Albeit messy at times, our dances are usually filled with fun and laughter. But here's the best part.

> **Let them praise his name with dancing and make music to him with timbrel and harp.**
> **—Psalm 149:3 (NIV)**

Every year, this group has a family Valentine's dinner and dance. For the first few years, Scott and I opted to not attend. Then finally, we decided we'd give it a try. During one of the songs, as I was dancing with Scott, I looked around the room and saw that each of our kids was dancing too. In that moment, I realized we were in the same gym where I attended those dances as a young, awkward teen. All of that longing, for all of those years, was being fulfilled—with my husband and our children. I was overwhelmed with God's love and filled with gratitude. The joyful experience that seemed to be so elusive just needed some time. In the end, it was even more beautiful than if it had come easily.

Ecclesiastes 3:4 tells us that there's a time for mourning and a time for dancing. We've had more than our fair share of mourning. You see, during that long season between our giving up the desire to dance and when we finally succeeded at it, we experienced deep grief. Our third daughter was born with trisomy 18, a fatal chromosomal abnormality. She lived for 2½ days, during which time we celebrated her brief life.

I got to hold her, rock her, sing to her, bathe her, and hear her faint cries. I got to be her mother. But as she left this earth for her heavenly destination, we ushered in all-consuming grief.

God has been faithful in offering His comfort and grace through our journey. He's helped us see meaning and beauty in our daughter's life. He's even restored our joy and laughter.

Along the way, I've come to think of grief as a sacred dance of joy and sorrow. The two are forever partners—joy for the love we have for our daughter intertwined with the sorrow of missing her.

It becomes sacred when we invite God into that space, because He can bring healing and hope.

God has shown me that grief is a reminder of our deep capacity to love. There is profound beauty in that. And so I embrace the grief. I try to sit with it and feel it instead of rushing it or ignoring it. As time passes, it walks alongside me quietly instead of being unruly and loud and disruptive. It truly is a sacred dance that has become more graceful over time.

We will forever miss our daughter, but we are choosing to dance until we see her again. I'm certain she's dancing too.

24 HOURS AND 54 MINUTES OF ANSWERED PRAYER

— By Eryn Lynum —

TEARS STING MY face.

Their hot sear on my skin is juxtaposed with the cold April breeze. I run into the wind, afraid I'm going nowhere at all.

The grief of miscarrying my fourth child is too much. I came here to run out the emotions and leave my anger and confusion on the trail, but it followed me right home.

It is my last run for a long time.

IT TAKES 3 years—three orbits of the earth around the sun—before I return to the trail to run.

I wake to an optimistic June morning in Colorado's front range. The summits of the Rocky Mountains are exposed by dawn's first light, glowing pink in the rising sun, their tips reflective and icy. The snow at their peaks will remain until late July, maybe August. I am grateful for the fair weather that coaxes my hesitant feet toward the trail. In 3 months, I'll be standing at the starting line of a mountain trail race, and it's time to train. The upcoming race is a small act of desperation, an attempt to convince myself to begin running again. Yet I sense there is a deeper reason I am taking out my running shoes after such a hiatus: my soul is aching for the restorative powers of nature.

My four children are still asleep—three boys we moved to these mountains with, and a daughter gifted to us last year, our "rainbow baby," a child in the wake of loss.

I leave them to their dreams, with Daddy asleep in the next room. Then, pulling on my sneakers, I step out into the chilly morning air.

> As for man, his days are like grass; like a flower of the field, so he flourishes. When the wind has passed over it, it is no more, and its place no longer knows about it.
> —Psalm 103:15-16 (NASB)

I gather my resolve at the trailhead, increase my pace, and run the first half mile uphill. It's a prelude—and a difficult one. It robs me of breath before the first mile marker. Yet as I push through short strides up the steep ascent and crest the initial lump in our foothills, I cannot gather my breath, for the view outright steals it from me. I don't know it yet, but my labored breath is a prayer. This initial run is the beginning of a liturgy; a request I'll lay at His feet each time I show up at this trail throughout the coming months. *Lord, take this broken heart and revive it with Your hope.*

The meadow below is alive with wild flax, the tall, slender stalks erupting into fragile blue petals. The lake is actively taking on the rising sun's reflection. The surrounding hills double themselves on the water's surface.

The trail dips down into the meadow and guides me along the lake's perimeter. I wind through a small patch of woods and emerge where the fishermen claim their places each morning along the beach or paddle boats out from the shore. They will always beat me to the trail throughout the summer, their habits formed long before my own. They're devoted to these waters. I push to dedicate myself as earnestly to the path.

As I pass them with a good-morning nod of the head, the trail takes me to the base of the foothills. I run parallel to the steep hillside, in and out of tall grass and beside the stretching branches of ponderosa pine. Eventually, the trail turns, leading me back up and over the hill toward the parking lot.

REPETITION IS A sort of salve to a grieving soul. Despite the temptation to stay in bed, I keep showing up at the trailhead. I have a feeling the resistance is not only a desire for an extra hour of sleep. Sometimes, healing must be fought for. It can be hard work. But to remain in bed might mean I miss out on an extra dose of God's new morning mercies today. I need to sense His presence out on that trail and to hear the whispers of His answer to my prayer.

With each mile, I discover consistent progress. At first, I don't even know that healing is what I am running toward. Yet each time I circle the lake, God is answering the raw and honest prayers of a mother burdened with loss.

Prayer isn't always audible. Sometimes it is a string of thoughts, an action, or a resolve in my spirit. I didn't know what exactly I was asking God to do out there on the trail. But I knew that He was sorting out my soul. He was acknowledging my grief and helping me to do the same, so I could then place it into His capable hands.

Back on the first day at this trail, I felt weak and battered. Yet with every consecutive run, it wasn't only my muscles that were strengthening, but my faith. Surrounded by creation, God reminded me He is the One who makes all things new.

I OBSERVE A performance of colors, aroma, and life unfold throughout the months. The bluebells are an opening act. Flax follows. Not long after, yucca stalks shoot toward the sky and blossom into a congregation of white flowers. Milkweed welcomes monarchs. Later into the summer, warmer days draw out delicious scents of sagebrush, honeysuckle, and juniper. My senses are alive with God's creation, and they're stirring something deep within my soul. In taking and giving turns throughout the seasons, these flowers have a way of keeping time. They assure me that God, although He is everlasting, has a time for everything.

My muscles strengthen throughout the summer, and with them, my spirit. I had hiked this particular trail a few times prior to this summer, but I had never spent so much time memorizing its details. By August, I know each turn of the path and every protruding rock to navigate around. Running becomes less of a trudge and more of a dance. It's less of an escape and more of a pursuit. Creation's songs beckon me through every hard mile. Hawks soar, hunt, dip, and cry from the open sky. Sandpipers probe their slender beaks at the water's edge in search of breakfast. The trees are alive with brightly colored warblers that come from afar, here on summer vacation.

In nature's rhythms, something inside me begins to revive. The plants and wildlife here seem to know, as I do, that new life does not negate lost life. Loss is always loss. Yet they dare to hope. In the sun's daily journey across the sky and in the rest and refuge of moonlight, this land follows its God-given directives, and in so doing, lives and breathes God's new morning mercies.

"Behold, I am doing a new thing." The words from Isaiah 43:19 (ESV) become a mantra on that trail. "Now it springs forth, do you not perceive it? I will make a way in the wilderness and rivers in the desert."

I run through the wilderness and the desert. It seems God calls His children to these places to grow their faith. Yet there is always a spring. There is always living water waiting for us. God is timely in this work, never piercing open the spring of water too early or carving a path for the river too late.

I'VE RUN 96.54 miles by summer's end, given 24 hours and 54 minutes to the trail. Over the span of an entire day, stretched out over 3 months, God has shifted something in my soul. Thinking back to creation in the garden of Eden, it seems right along with His character to perform wondrous, life-giving acts in the time frame of a day.

These numbers mean nothing to my Maker, who stands outside the confines of time. God measures things differently than I do. Yet, He often uses the limits of time to teach me valuable lessons and to grow me in His grace. Each step on the trail and every minute in His creation has revived my spirit.

In September, as I cross the finish line of my race, I discover God's answer to my prayer. He has healed my broken heart and convinced me that I am defined not by the losses of life but by His enduring hope.

I know there is more loss ahead. This broken world is riddled with it. Seasons of heartache are inevitable. Yet as Colorado's green grass turns to yellow and the last of the wildflowers lie low, their epilogue is a promise: there are good things to come. God is constantly at work. In every season, He grows our faith and brings new life. He restores joy to our steps and hope to our hearts that we, too, like the wildflowers, will rise again.

CHAPTER
4

FINDING THE RIGHT TIME AND WAY

ECCLESIASTES 3:5

A time to cast away stones,
and a time to gather stones together
a time to embrace,
and a time to refrain from embracing

INTRODUCTION

Stories about knowing when to hold on and when to let go

— By Shirley Raye Redmond —

CHANGE CAN SOMETIMES be frightening. The bigger the change, the more frightening it can be. Hannah More's life (1745-1833) was one full of changes—some exhilarating, as her talent for words catapulted her into the spotlight, and some disappointing and difficult, such as giving up her dreams of marriage and having children of her own. Because of her faith in God, and through His grace, Hannah stepped boldly forward into those changes. By doing so, she helped to change the world.

Hannah was one of five daughters born to Jacob and Mary More in England. Theirs was a modest, simple household, but the More sisters were brilliant, and Hannah outshone them all. She wrote her first successful play at the age of 18. It was performed locally and well received. Some years later, Hannah's quiet, sheltered life as an exuberant educator of young children came to a halt when she was invited to present her witty plays on the London stage. Almost overnight, Hannah became a pampered celebrity. She also wrote books in a wide range of genres, from inspiring tales such as *The Shepherd of Salisbury Plain* and her best-selling novel *Coelebs in Search of a Wife* to religious devotionals offering words of wisdom and hope. Hannah became a popular household name and one of the most-read authors of her time.

Although she received proposals of marriage, and at one time had eagerly looked forward to becoming a wife and mother, Hannah eventually changed her mind. She realized that her desire to provide education for the poor meant more to her than romance and marriage. Hannah chose to devote herself to her charity projects. Then in 1787, she met pastor John Newton—a former slave trader—and British politician William Wilberforce. Mesmerized by their passion for freeing the slaves, Hannah joined Wilberforce, Newton, and other Christian evangelicals determined to abolish the slave trade throughout the British Empire.

Hannah threw herself wholeheartedly into the cause, using her fame and social connections to win important supporters to the abolition movement and helping in the day-to-day running of a major abolitionist society. She wrote persuasively to awaken her countrymen to the plight of the African slaves, including the influential poem "Slavery," published in 1788.

Hannah and Wilberforce's goal was achieved in 1807, when Parliament passed a law to abolish slavery in the British Empire. Hannah died at age 87 in 1833, only a few weeks after her friend Wilberforce.

IN HANNAH MORE we have an example of someone who worked hard to "cast out the stones" of outdated attitudes and institutions in need of change, and who chose to embrace her faith and her convictions instead of chasing more wealth and social position. In the following chapter you will read encouraging stories about those who boldly leaned into life changes—moving into new homes, seeking out new jobs, learning how prayer and patience can bring the right person into your life just when you need them. They learned when to embrace new circumstances and when to let things go, and, most important of all, when to trust in God's providence.

A time to cast
away, and a
time to gather

A BINGO CHRISTMAS

— By Roberta Messner —

WHEN I ENTERED room 106 at Pleasant Hill Nursing
Home that December Tuesday, my friend's face was the picture
of disappointment. The moment Alice saw me, she said: "I never
thought I'd be living in a place like this, Roberta. All there is to do
is watch TV and play bingo." Alice shook her head at her tiny new
quarters. "I guess I don't have a choice. There won't be anything left
after they sell my house and everything. It's taking every penny to
pay for my care here."

I knew my friend was talking about more than boredom in a
nursing home. More than having no money too. Alice's greatest
joy in life came from showering those she loved with presents.
December was her very favorite month of the year for that.

Just then, Alice's nurse Katie entered the room with her
medication cart. "Did someone say bingo?" she asked. "There's a
bingo party after dinner this evening. Seven p.m. in the activities
room."

"Bingo?" Alice said incredulously. "I haven't played that since I
was eight years old and my brother and I went to the carnival. Used
hard kernels of corn for markers. Didn't win a thing then, and don't
expect to now."

Katie leaned in closer to my friend and spoke in a confidential whisper: "Fortune is on your side, Alice. You're talking to the Bingo Queen. Here's the deal. I'll wheel you down there and pick out your card. That way, you're sure to win." As Katie left the room, she added: "This is the night for the Catholics to host. They do love their bingo. And talk about treats and prizes. You never saw the like."

Alice (Mrs. Claus to those who knew her generosity) had transferred to the nursing home 3 weeks before, after several touch-and-go months in the hospital. Because of lung problems, she'd had to go to a special facility in Piketon, Ohio, 2 hours away from the cozy old neighborhood we'd shared in West Virginia.

My mother always told me one of the first sounds I ever heard was Alice cooing to me when they brought me home from the hospital. Alice promised we'd have great Christmases together when I got a little older. And how we had! I recalled the words Alice said to me every Christmas season, from her favorite book, *Little Women*: "Christmas won't be Christmas without any presents." Then she'd cackle and wink and show me her completed mail-order requests for cheeses and nuts from Swiss Colony, juicy Bartlett pears from Harry & David, and roses to be delivered at planting time from Jackson & Perkins. Not to mention her flurry of magazine subscriptions so her dear ones could enjoy Christmas every day of the year.

Alice's gifts were for everyone on both sides of our block on Madison Avenue. The Curtis family next door, Tiny Tow down the street. The Maynards and Mrs. Gray across the way. And she'd never forget Billy Jenkins around the corner, who came home every evening from school and taught his dad what he'd learned that day. Alice, a retired art teacher, loved that.

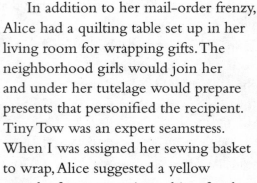

> By wisdom a house
> is built, and through
> understanding it
> is established.
> —Proverbs 24:3 (NIV)

In addition to her mail-order frenzy, Alice had a quilting table set up in her living room for wrapping gifts. The neighborhood girls would join her and under her tutelage would prepare presents that personified the recipient. Tiny Tow was an expert seamstress. When I was assigned her sewing basket to wrap, Alice suggested a yellow measuring tape for the ribbon and a fat tomato pin cushion for the bow. "Presentation is everything," she always told us.

How would the kind of Christmas Alice was used to ever happen in a place like this? Her only chance to afford presents for others this year was Katie and her not-too-promising "good fortune." Alice bit her bottom lip as a look of despair crossed her fragile features. The words that followed were as familiar as the icicles on her blue spruce tree back home. "Christmas won't be Christmas without any presents." But this year it wasn't a lighthearted joke she told while she rolled out her cart of festive wrapping paper and ribbons. It was heartbreakingly real.

I sent a quick petition heavenward that Alice would at least win *something*. But facts were facts. An Alice-Christmas was next to impossible. She begged me to stay for the dreaded bingo, and Katie steered her there in her wheelchair "Cadillac." When we arrived, we learned they were actually playing Christmas bingo, not the regular variety. Instead of numbers in the little squares on the cards, there were colorful holiday icons, like an old-fashioned gingerbread house, a candy cane, and a yuletide angel with glistening wings. Ol' Santa in his sleigh presided over the free space.

I tried to muster some enthusiasm. "This is great, Alice," I said, trying to convince myself as much as her. "It's a brand-new way to give!" When I managed to marvel at the cute little bingo cards, Alice caught the magic. "Try to find a card with Rudolph, Katie," she said excitedly. "I always put Rudolph stickers on my Christmas cards back home."

"Found it!" Katie announced. Then she rubbed the card to transfer good luck, squeezed Alice's shoulder, and returned to her nursing duties. That left me to be Alice's cheerleader. I scooted a metal fold-up chair close to her as the room filled with the more alert patients like my friend.

Up front, a lady dressed in a Santa's Helper outfit, complete with a holly-patterned apron, told the crowd they'd be using peppermint candies for markers. A young man in jeans passed around a plastic bag of the cellophane-wrapped delights. Everyone murmured their appreciation and declared they'd eat them later when they returned to their rooms.

Santa's Helper sang out, "We need a little Christmas, right this very minute . . . " Then she chirped: "Hello, folks! We *do* need a little Christmas here tonight. Everyone agree?" When Alice didn't answer, I positioned her card on the table in front of her wheelchair and forced a smile. How would she ever find something to love in this place?

The first Santa's Helper call was N-Christmas tree. Alice squealed as she located it on her lucky card. Next it was O-poinsettia. Again, Alice found it on her card. When the lady announced B-toy drum and I-tin soldier, Alice grinned from ear to ear. "All I need is G-star, and I'll have me a straight-across win!" she whispered. No one seemed to hear her but me. I patted her wrist and assured her she'd do it.

Alice did win that game, and she could hardly believe her reward. A brand-new, forest-green throw from QVC she immediately earmarked for Tiny Tow. "We'll wrap it next time you come to visit, Roberta. I'll send it home by you. We can use the table where they deliver my meal trays to tape the paper." Alice's cheeks flushed with excitement. "My trach ties will work for ribbon. They're made of a nice-weight twill. I think I can even loop them to make a bow."

Thanks to Katie's touch, Alice won three more of the evening's ten bingo rounds. Her prizes included a gift card for Bob Evans—perfect for Mr. Curtis, who adored their chicken-fried steak; a box of Russell Stover candy she'd send to Mrs. Gray; and a giant teddy bear, a splendid surprise for my sister Rachael's little boy.

When the Catholics closed with an invitation to feast on hand-decorated sugar cookies iced by the children, Alice bubbled over with joy. "Katie said we'd have Christmas bingo every Tuesday night at seven till Santa comes," Alice told me, smiling at the notion. "No matter what." The Nazarenes would be there next week; the Methodists the following Tuesday.

God had answered my prayer in a way I'd never dreamed possible. Alice would be at bingo with jingle bells on her furry pink slippers. Christmas—and home sweet home—had arrived for Mrs. Claus.

**A time to cast
away, and a
time to gather**

THE UNEXPECTED WEDDING GOWN

— By Janet M. Bair —

"HOW COULD WE ever afford one of these wedding gowns?"
I exclaimed to my friend, as we looked through another bridal
magazine. She was helping her daughter plan a wedding, and we had
browsed through many magazines looking for the "perfect" dress.

"These gowns are gorgeous, but $5,000 for something that you
only wear once?" I added.

I had a hard time with the idea of those prices. My husband
is an English teacher, and we have always lived frugally. My friend
was paying $8,000 for her daughter's reception. I began to feel very
burdened by the thought of weddings for our two girls when the
time came. Where would that kind of money come from?

That time could come sooner than I expected. Our younger
daughter, Emily, had just left her job in the United States and moved
to Brazil to explore mission work. She was also seeking God's will
with her Brazilian boyfriend, whom she had met in Mozambique at a
mission school. They weren't engaged yet, but they were pretty serious.

Sometimes prayers are answered before they are even prayed.
Sometimes the Lord gives you something that you didn't even
know that you would need.

Our older daughter, Joanna, was busy starting up her own
Christian dance and acting studio. Her challenge was costuming. To

> And it shall come to pass, that before they call, I will answer; and while they are yet speaking, I will hear.
> —Isaiah 65:24 (KJV)

put on the plays she envisioned, she would need numerous costumes. Fabric can be expensive, and sewing costumes is time consuming and challenging.

One afternoon, she called me. "Mom, my friend just called and said to come over to this bridal store. They're opening their back inventory to local theater groups for free. I'm going right now to see what they have."

"That sounds interesting. Have fun!" I said.

About an hour later, she called me again. "Mom! You've got to come over here. They have the most *amazing* dresses, and they're giving them away *free*! I picked out so many beautiful gowns that they won't fit in my car! Can you come help me narrow things down?"

After driving to the next town, I was astonished at the store's back inventory. I saw racks and racks of vintage bridal gowns with their price tags still on them. There were rows and rows of fancy dresses for bridesmaids or the mother of the bride, plus men's wedding suits and dress shoes. It was incredible!

As I wandered down the rows, I fingered some of the luscious satin, brocade, lace, and velvet on the gowns that were never sold. How to decide?

My daughter has pulled costumes for numerous plays, including an off-Broadway show, so she knows how difficult it is to find the right color or tone of a dress for the play director. We sorted through what we thought she could use for costumes for future shows, keeping in mind the sizes of some of her students. Not an easy task. Of the fancy dresses, we decided to select things made of expensive fabrics, such as lace or velvet, that would be costly to purchase. We could remake the dresses as needed.

Then there were the rows and rows of wedding gowns to look at. The selection was amazing.

"Take a look at these. I grabbed three or four gowns that look like possibilities if Emily decides to get married," Joanna said.

One pristine white gown in particular was breathtaking. It had a beaded bodice and a full skirt that was exquisitely trimmed with lace and beading. It also had a gorgeous long train. The price tag said $1,000.

When we finally loaded everything into our two cars, the gowns barely fit. What a tremendous blessing and boost to my daughter's fledgling theater studio!

Later that night, Joanna messaged her sister, "If you two decide to get married, I have a few wedding gown choices for you!"

That was in February. At the end of March, Emily got engaged. As a young couple interested in mission work, the two didn't have the money or the inclination to rack up debt for a wedding. Since she could stay in Brazil on her visa for only 3 months at a time, they were married at the end of August, 5 months later.

The gown that had caught my eye fit Emily perfectly in length, so I didn't have to change the beaded lace hem. I only had to make a few slight alterations to get a perfect fit otherwise. I had thought about making her a wedding gown at one point if we needed to save money. But this gown was so amazingly exquisite and far more intricate than I could have ever sewn!

Only God knew Emily would *need* a wedding dress sooner than we thought—and He provided before we even asked.

A time to cast
away, and a
time to gather

WAITING FOR HIS WONDERS

— By Lucinda J. Rollings —

"NO!" MOM EXCLAIMED. This was the stock answer we received any time we asked if we could help my 90-year-old, widowed mother.

"What about painting the carport?" I questioned, noticing the many holes where woodpeckers had feasted. "It's looking pretty bad."

"I guess," she relented. That marked the first time she let us help her, and the beginning of us becoming more closely involved with her day-to-day activities

Mom had always been very strong-willed and independent. As we spent more time at her home, troubling things became evident. I saw signs of dementia and became concerned about her living alone. And she had problems with her hip.

"Mom, when was the last time you saw the doctor?" I asked.

"Two years ago," she replied.

I checked her medicine. "You're about out of your blood pressure pills. Isn't it time for another doctor's appointment?"

"No!"

Reluctantly, to get her medicine refilled, Mom called her doctor, then grumbled, "They won't give me my medicine unless I come in." Our next struggle was to get her required blood work done.

"No!"

With some sneaky moves on our part, she finally agreed. However, when a second test was needed—"No!"

The doctor evaluated Mom's dementia and determined that she could continue to live alone for a while. However, looking ahead, we tried getting Mom used to the idea of moving.

"No!"

Eventually, she did agree to visit a few places. We started with an independent living facility. It was small and well maintained; the staff was friendly and caring. If she moved there while she was still able to get around with no problem, then when needed, she could easily move into assisted living with all the amenities furnished—meals, laundry, cleaning.

After the tour, I was very impressed and joked, "Mom, it's almost like heaven!"

Amazingly, she liked it. However, when an apartment became available . . . "No! I want to live and die in my own home!" she exclaimed.

I sympathized and didn't push. She had lived there more than 40 years. She loved the outdoors, and the wooded, country setting was quiet and relaxing. We often ate outside on her tree-shaded deck, listening to birdsong and watching critters scamper. Walking around the yard as she cared for her many beautiful flowers was excellent exercise for her, and she had good neighbors.

My husband and I have been in God's "waiting room" many times. Some of them were difficult—one lasted 10 years! Those experiences taught us that we can never predict how long we'll have to wait for the right door to open. But when God does open doors, His purpose and plan are so abundantly amazing.

So we accepted that this was another waiting room experience. We would wait for another apartment to become available and pray that God would change Mom's mind.

As for God, his way is perfect.
—Psalm 18:30 (KJV)

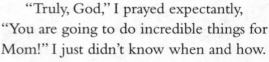

"Truly, God," I prayed expectantly, "You are going to do incredible things for Mom!" I just didn't know when and how.

Looking forward, I envisioned Mom enjoying life in her new, independent living apartment—the Bible studies she could join, the excursions, the gospel songfests.

However, reality with Mom at this point continued to be a different story of wins and losses. Mail was stacked everywhere in her house. Her kitchen cabinets and counters were so loaded with papers there was little room to prepare food.

Mom had trouble with her flip phone. "I can't get through," she'd moan.

"Let's get a landline put back in, Mom; it will be easier for you," I suggested.

"No!"

Driving 40 minutes one way to help Mom was not as much of a concern for us as our concern about her being home alone at night and not being able to use her phone correctly. She often left her doors unlocked. I went to bed every night praying, "Father, she is Your child. Please keep her safe and give me wisdom in her care."

As Mom's dementia worsened, I was in a quandary. My patience in God's waiting room dwindled. I bombarded heaven with my prayers.

Everyone was pushing: "Just move her. She won't like it at first, but she'll get over it."

However, it seemed to me that God kept saying, "Wait."

Then things began coming together. We had to deal with furnace, water heater, and plumbing problems, including a septic backup and a flooded basement. The house issues discouraged Mom, and she agreed to move. An apartment opened up, and the assisted living facility offered the first month rent-free. We started the process.

But then Mom cried, "No!"

I was so exasperated. Soothingly, God whispered again, "Wait."

Several times my devotions led me to Psalm 77:14 (KJV), "Thou art the God that doest wonders."

"Okay, Father, I'm waiting to see Your wonders," I prayed. And my faith walk s-t-r-e-t-c-h-e-d.

We took care of Mom and all her house issues during the Covid-19 pandemic. I praise the Lord for His protection in keeping us healthy. Covid-19 lockdowns devastated people in assisted living facilities and nursing homes, their families, and those who cared for them. Because I had followed God's leading to "wait," Mom wasn't there.

Mom was able to enjoy life in her own home until she fell and was taken to the hospital. She was in hospital care less than 24 hours when our Heavenly Father lovingly took her home. Instead of living in the apartment that I told Mom was "almost like heaven," today Mom is rejoicing in the real thing. After struggling through another season in God's waiting room, we saw that God truly did His wonders.

FINDING MY WAY HOME

— By Laura Bailey —

THREE DAYS HAD passed, and I still couldn't get out of bed. Calling in sick again wasn't an option, but the thought of facing another day made me nauseous. Today was the day. I couldn't put it off any longer. It was time to go home.

It had been only a year since I'd arrived in Montreal, thousands of miles from home, a recent college graduate, relishing my newfound freedom. I thought moving miles away would finally grant me inner peace and constant euphoria. But the newness had worn off and the excitement had waned. My life began to feel more mundane than magical.

When I was living at home, I'd felt suffocated by my parent's strict religious rules. Christianity was a list of dos and don'ts holding me back from having fun and being accountable to no one. But as I sat all alone in my apartment with tear-stained cheeks, I realized that I hadn't found freedom in rejecting my faith, but rather a deep emptiness and utter despair. I felt disconnected from everyone around me, ungrounded, and in constant turmoil. The feeling that this is not where I was meant to be had never stopped growing.

Pulling myself from underneath the covers, I began practicing for the conversations I needed to have that day with my boss, my boyfriend, and then my parents. I dreaded all three, but I knew the one with my parents would be the most difficult. Afraid of losing courage, I quickly dressed, decided to forgo breakfast, and headed toward the office.

MY LEGS BOUNCED. My manager had gone to refill his coffee cup and asked me to wait in his office. My palms began to moisten, and my heart raced. I scanned the room and made a note of where the trash can was, just in case. When my manager returned, I explained that I had decided to return to the States but didn't have the financial means to leave immediately. I desired to work another 3 months and earn enough money for moving expenses. It was a bold request, but he graciously agreed. As I walked out of his office, I couldn't help but feel the weight of failure. My dreams of living as an expatriate were dashed.

I sat across from my boyfriend at dinner, where tears quickly grew into anger; he felt betrayed, tricked, and deeply hurt. We had plans; how could I leave Montreal, and, more important, how could I leave him? I watched in pain as he walked away. His harsh words had been like salt poured in a gaping wound.

Lastly, I called my parents. I needed to ask them for their help in transitioning back home. I would need a place to stay, a new car, and financial assistance until I secured a job. My pride deeply wounded, I mumbled my way through the request. I pleaded for them to let me come home now, but they reminded me of my promise to my boss and encouraged me to take some time to think about my next steps.

Hanging up the phone, a mix of emotions wrapped around me like a blanket. Relief, confusion, anger, hurt, shame, excitement, and thankfulness ping-ponged through my thoughts. Muscle memory pulled my knees to the floor, and I began to pray. I'd been wrestling

> If you return to the Almighty, you will be restored: If you remove the wickedness far from your tent and assign your nuggets to the dust ... then the Almighty will be your gold.
> —Job 22:23-25 (NIV)

with God, not just for the last 12 months, but for the past few years. At that moment, I felt God speaking to my heart. While God didn't desire for me to rebel against Him, God allowed my experience in Montreal—my attempt to leave my faith behind—to move me to this exact moment of surrender.

In God's wisdom, He used my acts of disobedience to humble and transform me, so that I was no longer living my life from an earthly perspective but from an eternal one. God allowed me to "touch the hot stove of life" but saved me before I did anything that I would regret deeply.

The last few months in Montreal were emotionally and spiritually challenging. I was often by myself, but I always felt God's presence.

A FEW WEEKS after I'd returned home, I was still jobless, and I began to question whether I'd made the right decision. But God graciously confirmed I was right where He wanted me. In a chance meeting, I reconnected with an old boyfriend from college. He was from a small town, and he dreamed of living on farmland close to his family. His desires were simple: serve the Lord, work hard, love his family, and take care of his community. When I was younger, I turned up my nose at such a "simple-minded" way of living, but the idea of a quiet life didn't sound so bad anymore.

We are now married, living on 25 acres with our 3 girls, only 5 miles from family. It is an entirely different life than I'd imagined, but it's better than anything I could have planned. I stay at home with my daughters and am active in my church, writing and speaking about God's abundance of grace and His infinite mercy.

I've had the opportunity to share about my time in Montreal numerous times. God has placed young women in my life who are plagued with inner turmoil and conflict. They feel Christianity steals their freedom and think abandoning their faith is the solution to all their problems. I share my story with them, and I always smile when their eyes widen and they say, "Wait, you? But you are a good Christian." I am quick to remind them what they see today is the result of God transforming my life, at just the right time. It wasn't until I'd reached my lowest point that I understood—my way leads to destruction, but God's way leads to life.

I've spent many hours reminiscing about time lost due to my rebellion and waywardness. I think about the time I could have had with my husband—the season of isolation from friends and family—and I can't help but succumb to feelings of regret and remorse. But it was because of that season I turned to God. He knew that it would take me being at my lowest point to open my heart and surrender my life to His plan. God changed the whole trajectory of my life, and He continues to use my story to share the power of the gospel to change lives and bring Him glory!

LEARNING TO HUG, COVID-STYLE

— By Jennie Ivey —

THE LINE OF cars snaked around the store parking lot and stretched almost into the street. We were all there for the same reason—to safely pick up grocery orders that had been placed online. Before the pandemic hit, I'd always enjoyed shopping. It gave me a chance to get out of the house, to take in the sights and sounds and smells of a well-stocked supermarket, and—best of all—to exchange pleasantries, and often a hug, with friends and neighbors who were shopping too. Now, many of us were too nervous about the deadly Covid-19 virus to shop in person. There seemed little choice but to sit in endless, slow-moving lines to get the things we needed. With windows rolled up tight, I listened to the radio and played a game on my cell phone until it was my turn to pop open the trunk and have my groceries placed quickly and efficiently inside.

UNTIL THE PANDEMIC hit, I'd never heard of such a thing as "parking lot church." Now I was attending worship services from inside my car. With Covid-19 ravaging the nation, my congregation—like most others across the country—was forgoing services in the sanctuary. Instead, we gathered in the church parking lot, careful to position our vehicles a respectable distance from each other. Through the wonders of modern technology, the pastor's words came through the car radio. On Sunday mornings, I listened with gratitude as she read Scripture and prayed. I was renewed and uplifted by her sermons. And I sang, with as much gusto as I could muster, the old familiar hymns. I smiled at my fellow parishioners through the windshield. We beeped our car horns and waved to one another as we entered and exited the parking lot. Church like this was far better than no church at all. But what I missed desperately was the Passing of the Peace. "The peace of Christ be with you," we used to say in greeting those near us in the pew. "And also with you," they would answer. Then came the hugs. That's what I longed for most of all.

BECAUSE OF COVID-19, I hadn't seen my children or grandchildren in person in months. Sure, we FaceTimed occasionally on our cell phones, but it was never very satisfying. The grandkids either froze up or were much more interested in running around and playing than in carrying on a small-screen conversation. Who could blame them? All of them lived too far away to make socially distant meetups workable. Besides, I wasn't sure I was emotionally tough enough to see them without hugging them.

MY DAILY PRAYERS, which had once been deep and sometimes lengthy conversations with God, were now often reduced to just one question: *Why, Lord? Why must I live during a global pandemic?* If God answered, I didn't hear Him.

> For our light and momentary troubles are achieving for us an eternal glory that far outweighs them all.
> —2 Corinthians 4:17 (NIV)

One morning, while scrounging through an end table drawer looking for a pencil, I spotted my Bible. Before Covid-19 turned the world upside down, I'd read that Bible every day, no matter how busy my schedule. I don't know why I'd quit, but I had. The Bible had an attached satin ribbon I used for a bookmark, so I opened it there. Ah. Months ago, I'd left off reading in the book of Esther. Perhaps that was as good a place as any to start back. In chapter 4, verse 14, I came upon these words: "And who knows, you may have been chosen . . . for just such a time as this" (NCV).

Wow. This old, old story was written about a Hebrew woman who became queen of Persia. But might those words of encouragement for her be aimed at twenty-first-century me too? Were there ways I could show bravery during these terrifying times? Were there ways I could spread compassion and love?

I closed the Bible and closed my eyes in prayer. But instead of *Why,* I asked *How? How can I help during a global pandemic?* God's answer was short and simple: *Keep hugging.*

I thought back to the days when my three children were young. I'd figured out how to throw hugs to them by crossing my arms over my chest—right hand on left shoulder and left hand on right—and then flinging them wide. Thrown hugs saved time when we were in a hurry. They helped avoid embarrassment when the kids didn't want to be hugged in public. Could these no-touch hugs be of comfort during a pandemic? There was only one way to find out.

The next morning, I pulled on my walking shoes and headed outside. I spotted my elderly neighbor making her way gingerly down her steep driveway to retrieve the newspaper. "Stay put," I hollered. "I'll get it." I picked up the paper and tossed it at her feet. Wordlessly, she crossed her arms over her chest—right hand on left shoulder and left hand on right—and then flung them toward me. "You throw hugs?" I asked.

She nodded. "I've been doing it all my life!"

I wrapped that thrown hug around me and set off down the block. I threw it to two girls playing basketball on their driveway. "It's a Covid hug," I shouted. "Pass it on!" They both gave me a thumbs-up. On and on I went, sharing smiles and flinging hugs at my neighbors. Everybody who caught one smiled back and promised to not keep the hugs to themselves. That afternoon, I threw a hug to the teenage boy who loaded groceries into the trunk of my car. I threw hugs to my fellow parishioners the next Sunday during parking-lot church. And I set up a Zoom meeting with all my kids and grandkids. The first and last order of business? Hug-throwing.

Is a Covid hug just as wonderful as wrapping your arms tight around someone you love? Absolutely not. But it's a way to show love nonetheless. Given the choice, none of us would have wished to live during a global pandemic. But I believe God had a hand in putting me and countless others exactly where we were in this unforgettable time—just like He placed Queen Esther—to remind us to think of ways to stay connected, no matter what the circumstances.

We had to refrain from embracing. But that didn't, thank goodness, keep us from hugging each other.

A time to
embrace, and a
time to refrain

ENGAGED FOR A DAY AND MARRIED FOR LIFE

— By April Strauch —

NOT A DAISY was safe from my 10-year-old fingers as I plucked the delicate petals, saying, "He loves me, he loves me not." The desire in my heart to find my soulmate began that early. I can't remember a time when my biggest dream wasn't to become a wife. From my fifth-grade crush through two heartbreaking high-school relationships, I asked God, "Is he the one?" My friends made fun of me, but I didn't care. We each get dreams, and this was mine. I was undaunted.

By 19, I felt like time was running out. Mom and Dad were married at ages 20 and 22, so I assumed my time frame would be similar. Yet I was so hurt from my dating life thus far that, by my sophomore year in college, I had decided to take a break from "the dream." Besides, I'd been told by my youth pastor's wife, a woman I'd known and trusted since childhood, that I was too picky when it came to choosing young men to date. I started to believe her. If my relationships hadn't worked out, perhaps it was because I was too hard on others, expected too much.

Then I met Jacob. He was funny, exciting, and unlike anyone I'd ever met. Our backgrounds were clearly different, and yet we had so much fun hanging out in groups on campus. We'd talk and joke around for hours. He made me feel lighter, more carefree. Jacob told me that my listening ear helped him to sort through his complicated family dynamics. Although cautious, I soon wondered, *Will our relationship turn into something more than friendship?*

Indeed, it did. For 2½ years we dated. Looking back now, I see the red flags waving, but at the time Jacob and I embraced the good feelings and charged ahead. *Seize the day* was our attitude. For the longest time we had fun together, always laughing. However, when we started to think about a future together, the problems became obvious. He longed for city living; I'm a country girl to the core. Career came first for him; family was my heart's desire. His mother never accepted me; she made it clear to her only child that she wanted him with someone more cultured than me. Doubts grew as big as the mountains in my rural hometown. *Too picky,* I told myself, and brushed off my misgivings.

Then came a yearlong adventure for me in the Cayman Islands. The summer after graduating from college, I moved there to be a secretary at Triple C School. Before I left home, Jacob and I listened to our gut instincts about the cracks in our relationship and broke up. Through tears, we agreed that a fresh start was the right thing to do for both of us.

Within 6 weeks of moving to the Caymans, I felt at peace. I loved my job working with the kids in the school grades kindergarten to twelve, learning a new culture, and trying native cuisine. The principal was a middle-aged Caymanian woman who made me feel needed and appreciated. Cruise ships docked outside my apartment, where I gazed at them through the sliding-glass door and took pictures while I walked on the beach. I spent hours in a hammock dreaming of my future.

Despite my misgivings, Jacob wanted to remain in touch. Even though we'd agreed to a clean break, talking every now and then

> **Have I not commanded you? Be strong and courageous. Do not be afraid; do not be discouraged, for the LORD your God will be with you wherever you go.**
> **—Joshua 1:9 (NIV)**

seemed okay. Besides, the turmoil I felt when we were together in Pennsylvania was gone. Jacob told me he was enjoying his senior year as an economics major. As my insides continued to unwind, I had a deep sense of peace that we had made the right decision to move on. My story wasn't like I'd pictured; I wouldn't be married young like my parents. But I was content with the adventure God was writing. It was clear to me Jacob and I were only meant to be chapters in each other's life story, not the whole book. Soon, however, my faith was tested.

Jacob called to announce what he thought was a great surprise: he'd booked a flight for the very next day. He said he missed me and wanted to see where I lived. The next 24 hours were a blur. He arrived, and before I could blink, he took me to the gazebo by my apartment and got down on one knee with a heart-shaped diamond in a little velvet box. Every concern vanished for the moment it took Jacob to put the ring on my left hand. In the fleeting moment of that proposal, I rationalized that if Jacob cared enough to buy me a ring and make the trip to see me, my doubts about our relationship were unfounded. I quickly convinced myself the tangibility of the diamond—solid evidence of his willingness to commit—proved we could truly be happy together.

By the next day, however, fear and confusion emerged center stage. I went to work with the diamond facing my palm, so my coworkers wouldn't see it.

"Why didn't you tell me you loved me when you proposed?" I asked Jacob gently that afternoon. Truth was, he'd never said the words to me.

He simply replied, "Well, I guess I figured you would know that." But I noticed that he didn't seem upset that I'd never told him those words either.

It was hard when I returned the ring to Jacob the next day and sent him home, but my peace returned quickly. Mom always told me, "When in doubt, don't." Waiting for God's best was hard. But I had to trust it was worth it.

WHILE I WAS recovering my equilibrium in the islands, back in Pennsylvania, in the small country church my family had attended most of my life, sat a young man named Allen. We'd always been friends, but when I was 18, dreaming of a husband, Allen was 15 and couldn't drive yet. Not legally, that is. Tractors were always a part of his childhood on the family farm.

Word of my engagement spread quickly in the week between Jacob telling my family and friends of his intentions for our future and the next Sunday morning service. In a church the size of ours, it only took one person knowing a piece of news before a handful of the sixty-plus people in the congregation felt they were "in the know." Once a bell rings it can't be unrung. "April's engaged!" But only my family knew that it was now off! It was the custom in our church to share joys and concerns each Sunday morning. When it came time for the joys, the week of my "engagement," there was an assumption of a forthcoming announcement from my father. When the pastor asked him right out if he had anything to say, Dad calmly and succinctly said,

So do not throw away your confidence; it will be richly rewarded.

—Hebrews 10:35 (NIV)

"Nope." Allen froze, puzzled. After church, Dad explained to Allen, "April called it off."

Allen wasn't at all upset. Unbeknownst to me, he had been praying prayers of his own.

Several months later, my assignment ended in the Caymans. I moved back home. I was different than when I'd left. Before my experience with Jacob, I was an open book, sharing my hopes and dreams about love and marriage as a way of encouraging others to hang on to theirs, to never give up. Now, I was cautious, guarded. Although I remained confident in my decision not to marry Jacob, my dream of marriage was bruised and buried so deep I didn't even want to talk about it. The disappointments I'd faced in my love life were too many to remain optimistic that I'd ever find my true love. I asked God to help me accept that my plan just wasn't meant to be.

I'd been home from the Caymans for a short while when Dad called Allen and asked him to come and help move a mattress. While it was raining! When Mom questioned the timing, Dad answered with a twinkle in his eye, "We have to get Allen over here somehow!"

By the end of the day, Allen and I were giggling like teenagers. Over the coming months, my brain and heart couldn't fathom what was happening. This young man and I had attended the same high school and went to Sunday School together. When we were young, Allen's father would invite my family over for homemade ice cream. I'd noticed him from afar literally all my life, but because of the age difference we'd never run in the same social circles. Now, Allen became my world. Every time we were together, it just felt right. "Home" went beyond the location of the small town and house

I grew up in. We were falling in love. Dare I hope this was what I'd been praying about since I was 10 years old?

A little less than a year later, Allen proposed. He invited me to his house for dinner one summer evening. He had planned and prepared, with his mother's help, all my favorite foods. Down on one knee in the 150-year-old farmhouse he grew up in, he took my breath away. There was no question of what we felt for each other. Words came freely from both of us.

"I love you."

Twenty-nine anniversaries have passed. I absolutely know I wasn't too picky. There's no one else I'd want to go through life with. We have enjoyed and weathered the ups and downs that most certainly come for every couple: Owning a business, change of career paths. Dream vacation to Hawaii. Miscarriages, infertility. Two beautiful daughters born in faraway China. All of it—God knew who I was supposed to experience everything with. I'm beyond grateful that I waited for God's plan. No regrets, just more thankfulness than one heart can hold.

CHAPTER
5

RELEASING WHAT ISN'T NEEDED

ECCLESIASTES 3:6

A time to get,
and a time to lose;
a time to keep,
and a time to cast away

INTRODUCTION

Stories of losses large and small, knowing when to purposefully let go, and the blessings that came after

— By Shirley Raye Redmond —

JOSEFINA "JOEY" GUERRERO (1917–1996) knew all about coping with loss—both big and small. A vivacious Filipina woman living in Manila, Joey had been educated in a convent as a girl. She loved poetry and classical music and admired Joan of Arc. She was happily married with a two-year-old daughter when she was unexpectedly diagnosed with leprosy. The gut-wrenching diagnosis turned Joey's life upside down. Friends and family deserted her. Joey's husband reluctantly left her, taking their little daughter with him.

Then World War II erupted, and the Japanese invaded the Philippines. Many of Joey's friends and neighbors were killed, while others were rounded up and herded to labor camps.

With a courage born of desperation, Joey joined the underground guerilla movement. At great risk to herself, she aided American troops in the Philippines—delivering secret dispatches and maps of Japanese machine gun turrets and munitions facilities. She smuggled rations and medical supplies to fighters hiding in the cemetery and nearby caves. Her efforts saved the lives of hundreds of American soldiers and those of her fellow countrymen who were fighting against the Japanese.

Because of their horrific fear of lepers, the Japanese soldiers never ventured near the leper community or the nearby cemeteries. They never searched Joey—whose skin was blotched with lesions— for contraband. They never confiscated food she'd handled. Her hated illness became a tool she could use to help others who desperately needed her.

But even after the war, though she continued to pray for healing, Joey was forced to live in the nearby leper community. When US Army chaplains found Joey living in the filth of the leprosarium, they asked Congress to bring Joey to the United States to be treated for Hansen's disease, even though the government had a law barring lepers from entering the United States.

In the meantime, the United States government recognized Joey's courageous efforts during the war. On May 29, 1948, General George Moore presented Joey with the Medal of Freedom with Silver Palm, an award created by President Truman to honor foreign civilians who had resisted occupation and saved American lives during the war.

Joey was finally granted a visa to enter the United States for treatment by special ruling of the US Attorney General. She was only 30 years old when she arrived at the Carville National Leprosarium in Louisiana. Finally, her prayers were answered. Joey was cured, and she was later granted permanent US residency and then citizenship. She was also reunited with her daughter, Cynthia, who by that time had married and become a mother herself.

Joey never became bitter. She maintained a hopeful spirit and a grateful heart, once saying, "It is a constant source of wonder and amazement to me the way people everywhere have given of their time and effort to make my yoke sweet."

IN THE FOLLOWING chapter, you'll find stories by people who—like Joey—survived big and small losses, who learned to cope with tragedy and find healing in the blessings that came their way. And sometimes, with God's leading, they found that letting go can be the greatest blessing of all.

A time to
get, and a
time to lose

A CHANGE OF HEART

— By Vicki Kuyper —

WHEN MY TWO children were small, I started a tradition of making heart-shaped potato rolls as part of our Colorado Christmas feast. The choice to make them was a practical one—the yeast-based dough from this specific recipe actually rose, which is not always a given when you're attempting to bake at high altitude like I was. That first potato roll Christmas, I decided to cut the rolls with a heart-shaped cookie cutter, just as a little reminder of how much I loved my family, and how much God loved us. From then on, the shape of the rolls was as important as the recipe.

The rolls became a family favorite for both Christmas and Thanksgiving. One year, our house was filled to the rafters with friends and family for a very informal Thanksgiving buffet. After everyone finished eating, my mother-in-law asked my elementary-school-age daughter how she liked the turkey.

"Didn't have any," Katrina replied.

"How about the cranberry sauce?" my mother-in-law asked.

"Didn't eat it."

"Potatoes and gravy?"

"Nope . . ."

"What *did* you eat?" my mother-in-law inquired.

"Six potato rolls!" Katrina said proudly.

As I said, the rolls were a big hit. Not only the heart-shaped potato rolls but hearts in general became a kind of touchstone for our family. When (in what now seems like a matter of moments) my children grew to adulthood and my husband and I moved from Colorado Springs to Phoenix, Arizona, we nicknamed our new guestroom the Heart Rock Café and Oasis. Since our children no longer lived with us, Mark and I talked briefly about downsizing but decided we wanted our new desert home to be big enough to host family, friends, and even strangers—anyone who needed a quiet haven where they could rest and reconnect with God.

A DECADE LATER, I was the one spending the night in the guest room. But as I tossed and turned that night, my mind racing and my tears flowing, I knew I would find no rest. My heart was broken into so many jagged pieces that I felt there was no chance it would ever fully heal.

That night, my husband had said he needed to speak to me. Then he started to weep. Mark's sobs were so deep he could barely talk. I held him close, trying to quell his tears, certain he'd been diagnosed with some terminal disease. But Mark wasn't dying. It was our marriage of 33 years that wouldn't survive the night.

Mark's news—at least to me—was that he was gay. He said he'd known before we were married, but that he loved me and had truly tried to make our relationship work. Now, for him, it no longer did. My whole life changed in that one minute. My past—our courtship, our wedding, the classes we'd taught at church on how to have a great marriage, the great marriage I thought we had—all felt like a lie. My dreams for the future, all of which involved growing old with my best friend, had to be rewritten.

FIVE YEARS LATER, I'd left the Heart Rock Café and Oasis behind, following a circuitous route back to Colorado Springs to help my son, Ryan, and his wife care for two young sisters they'd adopted out of foster care. My ex-husband and I, although residing in different states and having recently finalized our divorce, remained close friends. Family vacations still lived up to their name, embracing every member of our growing family, including four new grandchildren, one on the way, and Mark's new life partner, Matt. Life wasn't always easy or comfortable or grief-free. But that doesn't mean it wasn't good.

> Love never gives up on people. It never stops trusting, never loses hope, and never quits.
>
> —1 Corinthians 13:7 (ERV)

Christmas had become an especially bittersweet season for me. Once my favorite time of year, it was now a vivid reminder of how much had changed. Unsure of where I'd be living or how much room I'd have to store anything, I had bid farewell to the beautiful bentwood reindeer and the Mickey and Minnie Mouse carolers that used to grace our oversize front porch. As a family, we'd divided all the Christmas decorations we'd collected over the years between the four of us. I had yet to take my share out of its box.

My Christmas traditions of baking a birthday cake for Jesus and creating a flock of penguin appetizers out of olives and cream cheese both fell by the wayside. They felt like too much wasted time, energy, and expense, when there were already plenty of holiday treats to go around. I missed our family traditions, but mostly I missed my family. The way it used to be. Although I spent much of the holiday season in the company of my son, his wife, and my granddaughters, every festivity concluded the same way. I returned to my little townhome. Alone.

Something had to change. And, as always, the one thing I had control over changing was me. I asked God to help me begin again, and I felt His urging to resurrect a few traditions to help celebrate Jesus's birth. I purchased a Christmas tree. I unsealed the box of ornaments and cranked up the Christmas music. Then I decided to make potato rolls for the first time since I'd suddenly become single.

But before I could get started, I had to find that heart-shaped cookie cutter. I'd tried to locate it a year earlier, searching through the plastic bin of assorted kitchen gadgets I'd toted with me through my last three moves. I figured it had just ended up in some random box, in with linens or cleaning products or office supplies. But when I'd moved into my townhouse, right before Christmas, I'd decided this was my final move. This is the place I would officially call "home." So I'd unpacked every box.

> I'm going to give you a new heart, and I'm going to give you a new spirit within all of your deepest parts.
> —Ezekiel 36:26 (ISV)

Although I'd given boxes and boxes of my belongings away over the last few years, I felt certain I wouldn't have left that cookie cutter behind. That little metal heart held almost as many memories as my photo albums. I searched through every drawer, shelf, and plastic bin in the kitchen, but it was nowhere to be found. As my plans fell apart, so did I. Why go to all the trouble of making potato rolls if they were just going to be *round*?

That one little thing—the loss of an old, inexpensive cookie cutter—was all it took to reopen the floodgates of my tears. I began to sob, my heartbreak feeling as fresh and raw as it did the night Mark told me he was gay. It felt like one loss too many. I was tired of rebuilding from what felt like the ground up when I was already in my sixties. My friends were retiring and celebrating milestone anniversaries, while I was buckling under the weight of helping care for my young grandchildren and worrying how I would navigate the "golden years" on my own.

"What do I do?" I cried out to God through my tears.

Text Mark, was my heart's immediate reply.

Although my ex-husband and I remained close, I didn't want to bother him on Christmas Eve. After all, I chided myself, this whole cookie cutter meltdown was undoubtedly just a ridiculous overreaction. However, if I were honest with myself at that moment, the truth was that I didn't want to admit the depth of my own grief—make Mark feel as though I was trying to make him feel miserable just because I was.

Text Mark. The insistence to act felt even stronger than before. So, I grabbed my phone. I tried to keep it short and not too bittersweet. I simply wished Mark and Matt a merry Christmas Eve and explained I was attempting to make potato rolls, while lamenting the fact that they wouldn't be heart-shaped.

"Open my gift," was Mark's simple reply.

I went to the Christmas tree and retrieved the box I'd received from him earlier that week. I'd planned on opening Mark's gift with my son and his family the next morning, but perhaps a little surprise right now would lift my spirits. Inside the plain brown shipping box, I found several wrapped gifts. There were Pfeffernüsse, which had been my grandmother's favorite Christmas cookie (so it had also become mine) and a panettone, a fruited Christmas bread I'd enjoyed when I went to school in Italy during my sophomore year of college. But it was the little square box that held my true Christmas treasure: a set of four heart-shaped cookie cutters.

The tears started all over again. But this time they were sparked by joy. The perfect timing of the perfect gift was a reminder that although I lived alone, I wasn't on my own. I was loved, and known, by both God and my family.

It isn't always easy for others to understand how the relationship within our anything-but-cookie-cutter family continues to grow stronger and deeper through the years. Some days, I don't quite understand it myself. But love is always a work in progress, a choice we make more than an emotion we feel. A fairy-tale family, we're not. But when it comes to love, we have that in abundance.

A time to
get, and a
time to lose

THE WILDERNESS AND THE WAY

— By Steve Watkins —

THE MOVIE CAME to an emotional conclusion and the credits rolled. Quietly, in the security of a reclining chair where I'd stared blankly at ceilings and walls for 3 years, I wept.

But the wheels were already turning.

This obscure 2010 film titled *The Way* kindled a spark absent for years. Through the tears, I prayed for some way to experience the pilgrimage journey it recounted across northern Spain, not so much as a healing period—I already felt that coming on—but rather for directional wisdom. *What now, Lord? Where does it all go from here?* Those were the questions where I needed answers.

For 5 long years, every circumstance seemingly pointed to a soul-crushing reality that I might never write stories again. From the early years of junior high school, I'd made the most of my writer's gift, and it felt like a part of me. By 2008, I'd created a satisfying career as a veteran 20-year journalist and owned a small publishing company working alongside some of the most talented people I knew. But one day, everything changed.

They called it the Great Recession, and it completely blindsided me.

One day I was on the fast track to become president of the local chamber of commerce. The next, I found myself broke, ashamed, and completely without a vision. Recovering from a professional setback like this is difficult enough. Managing it through the empty spirit of chronic depression immensely magnifies it.

For 5 long years, I struggled with my personal and professional identity, praying for clarity on direction and timing and the slightest hint about God's future for me. Surely, He hadn't cast me aside.

Little did I know at the time that God was pointing the way out of this wilderness.

The Camino de Santiago is arguably the world's most ancient Christian pilgrimage. The "French Way," or the most common route that pilgrims take, extends 500 miles across Spain's Iberian Peninsula from Saint-Jean-Pied-du-Port, France, to Santiago de Compostela, Spain, where it is believed the remains of the apostle Saint James are buried. I'd become familiar with the Way and decided to make the journey with no more than a backpack and an extra pair of shoes, praying that somewhere along the way, I'd hear God's clear direction. If nothing else, I'd lose a few pounds.

It's not an easy trek.

Pilgrims traverse mountain ranges with long, desolate stretches of nothingness. Weather conditions may be gracious, or storms may pummel you with ice from the sky. Brokenhearted, lost, and wayward pilgrims have walked the Camino for a millennium, searching for life's most elusive answers.

And so, I went to the Camino with preconceived notions of how a pilgrim should act. I'd be quiet and reverent and wait patiently for God's voice. He would speak in His time; this much I knew.

On October 23, 8,000 miles from home, lost but hopeful in spirit, I took the first of a million and a half steps westward, just as thousands of seekers before me had done.

> In their hearts, humans plan their course, but the LORD establishes their steps.
>
> —Proverbs 16:9 (NIV)

It is a grueling first day climbing the rocky path over the Pyrenees mountain range and crossing the border from France into Spain. A 13-hour walk concluded in the first village, Roncesvalles, and despite weeks of simulated walking and training, when I took off my shoes and socks, I saw painful, bloody blisters, and my muscles were beyond tired. For the second time in my life—surpassed only by the experience of running a marathon 10 years earlier—I experienced depletion.

The pilgrim's life on the Way is a simple one. Eat. Sleep. Walk. Repeat. That's what you do. In fact, this is among its greatest appeals.

Early on, something quietly set itself at odds with my preconceived notions about walking quietly and reverently. This ancient footpath is filled with interesting people from around the world, and every single one has an interesting story to tell. The Way of Saint James is a storyteller's paradise. And in my determination to wait and listen for God's voice, I'd practically taken a vow of silence.

Just past Pamplona, Jeannick Guerin, a Frenchman who'd spent the last 20 years working in the Australian coal mines, fascinated me. The morning we met he'd just been shooed away from a local farmer's chicken coop when there was no room at the local *albergue*, a hostel for travelers. He'd started his journey hundreds of miles back in France. Jeannick had terminal lung cancer, and he had returned to his homeland to say goodbye.

Vegan Tom's compelling story of growing up during the fall of Polish communism came with a price. His judgmental attitude about things as trivial as drinking a Coke wore quickly on a weary soul who occasionally enjoyed typical American pleasures.

My transformation happened on day five, just a couple of miles east of the village known as Puenta la Reina. For the first time, I paused, turned around, and looked back to see where I'd been. A hundred miles down. You can anticipate this moment, but nothing prepares you.

It took my breath away. For the first moment in 6 years, I witnessed how far I'd come. So much progress. The Pyrenees were now a majestic piece of background on the distant landscape. I'd kept going through the pain and exhaustion. Didn't quit. Pressed on.

I'd never experienced more gratitude than in this moment and I fell to my knees and prayed this to God: "Dear Lord, thank You for bringing me to this place. I know that You are making a way for me as we speak. But Lord, there is a door I must walk through now, and I pray that if it's not Your will that You close that door before I pass to the other side. I am surrounded by stories, Lord, and they are good stories—the kind that can help people see You and Your holiness. I need to tell these stories so that others might see You through me. I need to be a storyteller again, and I believe this is Your will."

After 6 years lost in depression, questioning my own identity, and forgetting who God had made me to be, I had the answer to my prayers in the form of the stories that others shared with me. I was still a writer, still a storyteller, and, despite the blow that had taken me away from my publishing career, I knew I would find my way back to it, even if it took a different form. I became myself again. It took His time and the right place for Him to show me. And it took the initiative to walk the path alongside Him and listen. Taking that step—this is the heart of our faith and the chief attribute of His children.

Processing it all back home, I desired to make greater meaning of the experience. I dug out my daily notes from the walk and organized them. Though I'd never written a book, they resembled how I imagined chapters in a book. And so, I did the only thing I knew to do to get a further understanding of this journey: I wrote. For 2 years. Some of us only understand how we feel when we see the words in front of us, and somewhere in this writing experience it all became clear. The Camino had not been just a different sort of vacation, and it was more complex than a long walk. It was the way that God showed me how the most difficult times in our lives might be weaved into His purpose.

The book was not only published but won several literary awards, both national and international. In 2018, I spoke about the experience of finding myself on the Camino at seventy-three different venues from coast to coast. This became the opportunity of a lifetime, ministering to others who'd experienced a debilitating depression and nearly lost hope.

My heart gave up a dozen times through all this, but the Holy Spirit inside helped me take a small step forward every day. Finally, the time had been right for me to heal.

A WEIGHT LIFTED OFF

— By Elsa Kok Colopy —

IT STARTED INNOCENTLY enough. My daughter Samantha and I would go out for ice cream on a Saturday afternoon, run through the drive-through on a Friday night, or grab a quick snack from the gas station shelves as we ran around town. We were on our own, and the fast-paced life of single parenthood lent itself to meals on the run.

Looking back, I can see where we started leaning on food in more emotional ways. It was ice cream for a reward or even for comfort after a tough day. It was a meal out because "we deserved it after all that." Whatever "that" might be.

I began dating when Samantha was five, and when the relationship turned serious, she was excited. She was thrilled to have a fun-loving man in her life and had big hopes we would become a family. When the relationship didn't work out, her tender heart was broken. I remember holding her as she cried. "I thought he would be my daddy!" We both began to lean on food, and I could see the effects begin to impact my little girl. Her weight started to become an issue, and her self-esteem began to erode. She didn't like the look of the girl in the mirror. I would try to help her see her beauty, but she felt fat and began to dislike herself because of it. I felt helpless as a mom and upset with myself for the ways my decisions had impacted her heart.

Time passed. I had come to know Jesus at a new level, and my relationship with Him had come to the forefront. I felt His healing touch on my life, and my faith became real. I started writing and sharing about my faith, and my beautiful girl went on that journey with me.

Then life threw a curveball. A devastating blow knocked us both when I lost my dad in a sailing accident. My whole family flew to Florida for the funeral, and Samantha connected with her cousins through their grief. Three of the cousins had always been especially close. They were all the same age and always spent time together at family reunions. At the end of the time together, each family headed back home. Only 12 days after my dad's passing, my 17-year-old nephew Caleb was in a car accident and died instantly. Samantha, also 17, didn't know what to do with the heartache, with the depth of grief over the loss of her Opa and cousin. She gained more weight as she went to the same places she'd always known to find comfort. The painful truth about food issues is how the weight of shame gets tacked on. Something hurts, we eat for comfort, the shame comes and that hurts, so we eat more. I had seen it play out in my own life, and I now saw it in hers. I prayed. I asked God to heal us both.

Years passed. Samantha grew to adulthood and went through several more hard things. Each time her weight seemed to increase even more. Finally she had enough and asked if she could get some counseling. She worked hard. For 2 years she tackled some of the deep wounds that had put the weight on. The counseling wasn't a magic bullet, but it did help to set her up for health and success.

"I remember you were renewing a commitment to being healthy on April first," she told me. "It was the catalyst. After all the hard emotional work, I knew it was time. I was just sick and tired of living the way I had been living. I was done. I cut my calorie count and started going to the gym, and the pounds began to come off. First it was 5, then 10, then 20. I was so excited to share every pound lost with you. It was like unwrapping a gift when we celebrated each pound together!"

One evening Samantha was driving home. It was late at night, and she took an unfamiliar turn too wide. She went over the edge of the road and overcorrected. Her small coupe flipped a time and a half and landed on its roof. There she dangled, stunned, hanging upside down. Carefully, slowly, she wiggled out of her seat belt and through the window out onto the grass. Other than a scraped-up arm and a broken tailbone, she walked away unscathed. Her car, however, was totaled.

> . . . being confident of this, that he who began a good work in you will carry it on to completion until the day of Christ Jesus.
> —Philippians 1:6 (NIV)

"How?" she asked me, tears on her cheeks. "How could I possibly have just scraped my arm? The window was open, and my elbow was on the window's edge because the night was warm. And yet it just touched the asphalt enough to get a slight road burn? Wasn't broken? Wasn't smashed as the car rolled over and over?"

The next week, we went to go see the car. I had to gasp as I walked up to see the damage. The roof was crumpled in, the steering wheel was scrunched forward, and the space between it and the seat was inches wide. The window itself was bent in. My heart pounded with the sheer terror of what could have been. My baby, my girl. All could have so easily been lost. I knew the moment I saw the car that God had intervened and saved Samantha's life. She was exactly the right size to have survived. She still had enough weight that the steering wheel had kept her from slamming into the roof and breaking her neck. And yet she had lost just enough that her legs weren't crushed and she was able to get out of the car despite the crumpled roof and bent window.

Only a few months after the accident, Covid hit, and Samantha was infected. Her oxygen went down to dangerously low levels. Normal oxygen saturation ranges in the blood are between 95 and 100 percent. She was in the 70s at night as her body fought the hard hit of this pandemic. As with the car accident, if her weight had been at her original spot, she would never have survived the nighttime drops. The sheer volume of her body weight would have pressed too hard against her struggling lungs, inhibiting their ability to expand. On the other hand, if she had lost it all, she would not have qualified for the intravenously administered antibodies that ultimately turned the disease around.

After years of counseling, prayer, and the hard work of healing, God had prompted Samantha at just the right moment to save her life—two times in a single year.

Samantha has lost 105 pounds as of today and is still losing. She has a hundred pounds to go before she reaches her optimal weight, and she is pursuing health with renewed passion. She can so clearly see how God has protected her, directed her steps, and guarded her life by orchestrating every single detail of her journey. No detail was left unseen, no wound left untended. Like a loving Father, He has walked with her every step of the way, strengthening, sustaining, healing, and protecting—as only He can.

A time
to get, and a
time to lose

SURVIVING THE LOSS OF A BUSINESS

— By David L. Winters —

STERLING LOOKED OUT the window of his office at the neatly lined rows of trucks stretching out in front of him. Beginning with just one semi, his growing business now boasted eighteen trucks and a repair shop. As a significant transporter for General Motors (GM), his drivers hauled goods around the eastern half of the US and beyond. On each truck, he displayed a conspicuous testimony of faith—a logo with a cross and statement about the company's commitment to God. Blessings flowed.

Although Sterling funded the business expansion primarily on credit, the earning potential seemed limitless. With such a large, stable customer as the world's largest automaker, he added trucks and drivers every other month. At one point, it became difficult to get so many trucks serviced. After a few frustrating delays, Sterling bought a truck repair business, and used it to fix breakdowns and obtain maintenance for his own fleet—as well as trucks from other companies.

"Not bad for a country boy from Kentucky," Sterling said to his wife, Julie.

"God has truly blessed," she responded while wrapping an arm around her husband's waist. "Lots of time and effort went into building all this."

"Let's go grab some dinner at the steakhouse," he suggested.

The warm early summer breeze enticed Sterling and Julie to the restaurant's outdoor seating. Flower boxes around the perimeter of the seating area added subtle scents of springtime. A delicious meal and romantic conversation lent the evening an idyllic quality that belied the disaster awaiting the next day. The couple slept well that night, with no idea what the morning might bring.

Sterling's day always began with breakfast and news from a popular business channel. Julie served up pancakes and eggs as he fired up the television in their eat-in kitchen.

After a commercial break, the newscaster read a statement that would rock his world: "In news that shocked the stock market this morning, GM announced their bankruptcy filing, which is sure to ripple throughout the economy. The maker of such brands as Chevrolet and Cadillac will reorganize under Chapter 11. Declaring assets of $82 billion and $173 billion in liabilities, the firm insists it needs the flexibility of bankruptcy protection to remain solvent and continue employing tens of thousands of Americans."

"Oh my gosh, honey, what will this mean for the business?" Julie asked.

"I'm not sure, though it certainly won't be good."

"I thought the government just bailed GM out in December..."

He just stared at his wife. All the color drained from his face as he thought about the possibilities. Would he lose his business? Could they lose the house? Would the final chapter of his story be about the failure and demise of his company?

Sterling and several of his competitors had talked frequently about GM's money woes. Although the government had tried to prop up the giant car company with $17.4 billion in December of the previous year, the bailout must not have been enough. Changing economic conditions, including runaway inflation, significantly increased costs—and not just for the auto giant. Sterling himself found it increasingly difficult to bid accurately on transport jobs. Gasoline prices fluctuated by 10 to 15 percent from when bids were offered until loads were picked up. The change in price could turn a profitable route into a losing proposition. Bid too high, one of his competitors would win the contract. Bid too low, his own company would lose money.

> The blessing of the Lord makes one rich, And He adds no sorrow with it.
> —Proverbs 10:22 (NKJV)

Shock waves followed the bankruptcy announcement. For months, GM didn't pay its suppliers. The company's accountants prioritized parts makers over transportation companies. Many small firms like Sterling's were plunged into very difficult circumstances. Julie and Sterling determined to trust God and hang on until GM received an anticipated second bailout from the government.

In the meantime, his creditors grew nervous. The banks rattled sabers and called in loans on his trucks after very short periods of delinquency. One of the hardest days of his life was when he sold the first batch of trucks at discount prices, just to satisfy an antsy creditor. He hated to do it, but the bank required the sale; he had no other choice. Still, he prayed that God's will be done.

The hits kept coming as it became clear GM would not ever have to pay back firms like Sterling's. The automaker's debts were dissolved by the bankruptcy court. GM focused on retaining as many of its own employees and maintaining relationships with parts suppliers, which they would need to build cars in the future.

Sterling's fleet shrank from eighteen trucks to fourteen and eventually to just two semis. His business volume declined to a fraction of its recent size, and earnings plummeted. It felt like a gut punch. He and Julie tried to maintain the good fight of faith. They prayed many times, read God's Word, and hoped. On down days, he felt like a modern-day Job who saw his possessions quickly destroyed.

Several times, bitterness tried to creep in—such as when GM announced a multimillion-dollar bonus for the CEO who successfully led them through the bankruptcy. Julie reminded Sterling of God's love and the temporal nature of earthly possessions. He managed to rejoice that they weren't forced to sell their home or to make major lifestyle changes.

Finally, one particularly sunny day, Sterling and Julie again stood looking at the two trucks that now made up his fleet. Completely at peace, he prayed with words of thanksgiving. "Lord, thank You for guiding us through a difficult time. Your mercies sustained us as my dreams washed away like so much rainwater down a mountain. Now, we thank You for my continued ability to make a living, to pay for everything we need, and to give to your work through tithes and offerings."

That wasn't the last of Sterling's losses; a few years after the GM bankruptcy forced him to let go of so much that he had built, his beloved wife passed away from cancer. And once again, God provided: first time to mourn, and then a new wife to share his later years. Through seasons of abundant blessings and seasons of loss, Sterling learned that letting go can be among the sweetest of experiences—if we can find the comfort of God's love.

A time to
keep, and a time
to cast away

KEEP, TOSS, OR BURN

— By Donna K. Wallace —

I STOOD AT the tall windows of the chalet. The Spanish Peaks, deep in white and crowned with golden splendor, her bridal veil of fields crusted with diamonds, bowed and stepped back as a closing curtain of fog signaled another storm due to arrive. Springtime in the Rockies meant bluster, the drama playing out with daily precipitation in any number of frozen forms. Stunning.

And fearsome. The sheer magnitude of nature in Montana made me feel all the more obscure. Winds slammed the side of my little house set high on a hill. I shivered. I wanted to cry but couldn't find the energy. I put another log on the fire. My entire world was now enveloped in a cloud.

The thrill of life out on the lone frontier was not what brought us here. Married with two little children, I'd pressed toward what I believed God had called me to. I loved my current position as a university professor at a small Christian college, my alma mater, where many of my best friends were also employed, but it wasn't the academic path I'd started out on.

Years before, I'd been offered a full-ride scholarship to an Ivy League school for my PhD—my dream come true, though the pace of the busy metropolis and constant freeway traffic proved exhausting. I had just begun the program in tandem with adjunct teaching when I was diagnosed with a serious autoimmune disease. Each semester I became more overwhelmed under the burden of chronic fatigue and all-over body pain. *How can this be?* I wondered. This was my dream job. How could things have gone so wrong?

"You're losing yourself, and us," my husband had quietly said. One day, he gave me an ultimatum: the kids and him and a move to someplace where I could heal, or continue on that extremely demanding career path. He knew such a drastic measure was the only way to get my attention. He was right. I did not want a divorce, and I did want to be well again. When I stilled long enough to consider my immediate reality rather than lofty ideals, I realized no profession was worth losing all that I treasured most dearly. There was no 5-year stretch of marriage or our young children's upbringing that I wanted to miss.

But now, contemplating the stormy Montana sky, the choice of having left community and vocation seemed like a terrible mistake. I looked at a glossy new box of business cards sitting unopened on my library shelf with all my books. In my final months there, the college had transitioned to university status, and the faculty and staff were issued new shiny business cards with new titles. Now my library, my name cards, and my dreams were nothing but mementos. I had never even opened the box; my past title taunted me. Silly to have moved those cards here.

Had our move been too extreme? This loss of everything I'd hoped for couldn't possibly be God's plan.

I called Alison.

My best friend from the college I'd loved and left described her morning of sticky hands and hungry tummies of three sons under age three. Her dream of being a mother had come blissfully true in a landslide of sorts, but the cost had been high: she'd had to leave her role in admissions and move far away from our close community of friends. Though she adored being her little ones' mommy, she was discovering the downside of domestic life, namely lack of sleep and mounds of dishes and dirty diapers. And the incessant drumming of spring rain.

When the twins arrived, Alison realized she would not be able to return to the office, and her family moved to Sonoma, California. Soon after, my family began our journey to the wilderness of Montana. With my kids in school, the most pressing tasks of the day were to carve a path through deep snow to the firewood pile and wash skunk smell off the dog. The snow was flying sideways. The memories of the college community where Alison and I sprang to life as young women—the future potential of the roles we held—were mere dusty shadows.

Phone calls were expensive in 1998 and had to be kept to a minimum—which for us meant a once-a-month treat. After putting the boys down for a nap, Alison brewed a cup of tea, and we perched on stools where our phones connected to the wall, catching up on our kids' latest and mostly endearing and hilarious antics. We lamented and shared some wins and news about friends in common. Today, her boys fussed and fought sleep but remained corralled in their playpens long enough for Alison to stretch the red phone cord into her pantry where she could mostly close the door. She narrated all these things before pulling in a deep breath through her nose. "I smell like sour milk."

The phone line rustled as she crawled over to the laundry room in search of a fresh top. Her voice wavered. "I'd fall asleep right

> Strive for full restoration, encourage one another, be of one mind, live in peace. And the God of love and peace will be with you.
> –2 Corinthians 13:11 (NIV)

~

now if I didn't so desperately need to hear your voice telling me something intelligent about life beyond these walls."

That was laughable. I too mourned lecture halls full of open faces, syllabi, and social theory. I felt my friend's ache as sharply as my own etched into the wall of my heart, of that still-living and mysterious space, of a life and a dream slipping away.

"Maybe we should do what the prophet Isaiah wrote: 'Forget the former things; do not dwell on the past.'"

"Mhmm."

"'See, I am doing a new thing! God says' . . . which I might be able to see if it wasn't for the blizzard outside," I said with a note of humor. "'I am making a way in the wilderness and streams in the wasteland,'" I optimistically quoted Isaiah from memory.

Alison's fatigue had dug a hole of despondency. "Lord, if only you'd make a way through this wilderness of my kitchen," she petitioned with a big yawn. "I don't know, D., this is not what I envisioned for my life."

I listened while stoking the fire.

"I need to stop dwelling on the past," Alison said. "I go there to keep my sanity with the babies some days, to that life of a carefree college girl, with my whole life waiting with possibility." She let out a long sigh. "I just don't know how to take hold, what to keep, what to let go of so I might bring the chapters of my life together. Getting a degree was my emphatic 'Yes!' to God. I love my babies. But now what?"

"I have an idea," I said.

"READY? IT'S TIME."

I was met with a quiet, "Yes. I have mine."

"Is your fireplace lit?"

"Hot."

"Tissues?"

"Check."

I lifted the lid and set it aside. I pulled a card. We each read our previous titles aloud from raised, shiny blue font set against a textured white background to compliment the university's three-word mission, one we'd come to know as our own. Emblazoned on the image of a shield were: Truth. Virtue. Service. My box was still almost full. I ran my finger along the edges stacked tightly together, cards having never been slipped into a handshake. I shuffled a batch of the handsome business cards—four hundred and seventy-two anticipated phone calls, luncheons, and speaking engagements that now would never happen.

> May he remember all your sacrifices and accept your burnt offerings.
>
> —Psalm 20:3 (NIV)

With trembling fingers, we each lifted our offering and religiously held a handful before releasing the cards to our respective pyres, watching them ignite and curl in on themselves. Watching my dreams turning black around the edges, I wished I knew how to pray in Latin or even the lyrics of a sad Irish song. I didn't.

Alison began to openly sob across the phone line, which made me choke up too. Cycling through grief at turbo speed, I could no longer deny this loss, this fury, this sadness . . . positions that were no longer ours, form-fitting office wear and cute shoes a lifetime ago—several little lifetimes ago for Alison. I chucked more than half my cards in and watched sparks fly. Two hundred more to go.

I admired the one in my hand. "I felt loved and known there. And now I feel . . . erased."

"Me too," she whispered.

Feeling the weight of each loss on my fingertips, I flicked the remaining fraction one by one through the top of my red woodstove, watching the smoke and snow swirl together outside in the Rocky Mountain storm, hearing the hiss of each card stubbornly exploding into its tiny burst of flame.

Alison described tossing her cards into a fireplace much like a dealer would at a craps table, then chucking on a mound of soggy tissues. We were praying our goodbyes, and for the benediction we each did a two-handed toss of our pretty oblong card boxes into the flames.

"A time to keep, and a time to cast away," I said. I had no other words.

ON THAT SODDEN day long ago, Alison and I did not yet know this bright and difficult future of ours, the many invitations, these choices we'd make and how our children needed mothers to help navigate theirs too. We were merely letting go of the past, so that we might be free to take hold of what we'd been given. We didn't yet recognize how a deliberate act of laying down our hard-cast ideas of "vocation" allowed God to refine our calling, and that our relinquishing of title became a prayer in and of itself—a prayer that allowed us each to walk into our new circumstances or at least start changing how we felt about them.

We gently laugh now, not *at* our earlier selves, but while holding the memory of those young women in the arms of the protective mothers we grew to be. Neither of us had yet attained noteworthy status in our careers. We grieved something more pure, more innocent. This "way" in the wilderness, this "stream," came at great expense. On that day, we held what felt like concrete choices, the keeping and the casting away. And, though our positions had changed, our story of being called with special purpose did not.

We've each had several titles since, "Mama" being our favorite. Our kids are grown. I have a doctorate and very much enjoy teaching again. We've come to know that titles don't define us, only being God's beloved ones does. That is identity enough. Each morning we wake to a new space, as a new person in Christ, and we begin again. Frederick Buechner said, "What's lost is nothing to what's gained, and all the death there ever was, set next to life, would scarcely fill a cup. And yet, and yet: There remains the need— perhaps even the responsibility—to grieve."

I often think about how necessary ritual is, even when homespun like ours was, to allow one's hands to firmly grasp that which needs to be held, to feel the weight of it, to bless it and then let it go in the presence of a trusted friend. We recognize the burning of our business cards as the shared sacred ritual it was, one that helped us transition from one chapter of our stories to the next. The fact remains that the best of what those cards held are still with us, in us. Even across all these miles. All these years.

THE BABY-SITTERS CLUB

— By Ashley Kappel —

I HAVE ALWAYS loved to read. As a child, you'd often find me under the bleachers with a book while my siblings played basketball, toting a new novel along to the beach, or even sneaking comics during family dinners. My favorite series, The Baby-Sitters Club, boasted dozens of volumes, all of which I read repeatedly as I dreamed about being a big kid.

As the youngest of four, I often found myself somewhere not exactly against my will, but not of my choosing. Instead of long afternoons at home, we would crisscross the state to various gyms where my sister played basketball or fields where my brother starred as goalie on the soccer team. During those seemingly endless miles, I would thumb through my backpack and pull out a well-loved, almost-memorized story of a group of girls who got together to fill a need in their neighborhood and the adventures they had while doing it.

Eventually, I outgrew the series. I tried others, but nothing stuck. I bounced around from school reading to fiction without much taking. I would even occasionally sneak a chapter or two from my beloved books, now lined up perfectly across a shelf in my room. Like comfort food, but for the brain.

When I moved out of my childhood bedroom, my mom insisted on boxing up the hundred-plus books from the series I owned and packing them away in the attic. "Mom," I protested, "they're so beat up, and I'm not going to read them again." She nodded but kept scooching them back toward the boxes with Christmas decorations. "Someone else might," she said, cryptically. "You never know when you'll need something again. These were so special to you once; I bet they'll come in handy before you know it."

Years passed. I graduated college, moved to Birmingham, got married, bought a house, and started a family. Our home quickly filled with my weakness: Books. Board books, classics, poetry, and fairy tales filled our bedtime hours while actual shelves of books appeared in every room of our house.

Not long after my children were born, my mom decided to join us in Birmingham. As I was helping her move items in her attic, I noticed the old file box, the one neatly labeled "Ashley's Books."

"You still have these?" I asked, shocked that they had survived the great house culling and the move from 2 hours away. I pulled out one of the pale pink volumes, running my finger down its well-bent spine, where each book was numbered from one to well over one hundred. "Mom, we should find someone to give these to," I said, letting my eyes spill over the rainbow of books in the box. "We will," she replied. "Sometimes you have something and just know that God has a plan for it to be useful later."

Time passed. My children grew, and then the pandemic hit. We watched as our kids, then all under the age of seven, lost, well, everything. Their schools, the zoo, playdates, everything snapped closed with a foreboding and almost audible clang. When once we scuttled around to sports practices, lessons, and parks, we now busied ourselves with fun at home. Art projects covered our walls, water gun fights covered the front yard, and the kitchen saw more than a few dozen batches of chocolate chip cookies move through it. We were home, perhaps a bit stir-crazy, but healthy and mostly happy.

> And do not forget to
> do good and to share
> with others, for with
> such sacrifices
> God is pleased.
> —Hebrews 13:16 (NIV)
>
> ~

One day, a neighbor from up the street and his daughter were going on their daily walk. From our yard, I called out to the girl, Anna, asking her how she was doing. Anna, about nine, was a few years older than my daughter Olivia, and old enough to be quite sad about the things she could no longer do (instead of thrilled at the extra time at home, like my younger kids). She was quiet for a moment, then began to cry. "I just really miss the library," she said. Anna has always been a favorite neighbor kid of mine. She's beyond kind, always welcoming the younger kids to play when older kids might wish for more "big kid" games. She was a wonderful listener, asked bright questions, and really looked at you while she talked—truly, an old soul in size-5 sneakers. In the days since the lockdowns began, her little light had become a bit dimmer.

I felt a little twinge. "Do you read The Baby-Sitters Club?" I asked her. Her eyes lit up and her dad laughed. "She's read every one she can find!" he called out.

I called my mom to ask her if she was okay with me giving Anna the books. "They're your books," she said. "And now maybe they're hers."

I texted Anna's mom that afternoon: did she think Anna would like the books? I told her they were well loved, but the up side of that is she didn't need to worry about keeping them perfect.

"That would be incredible," she replied. "We've been praying for a way to lift her spirits and remind her of all the good that she still has; she will LOVE this." I could hardly believe how perfectly this was working out; who would have thought that the person I would save these books for—the girl whose parents had been praying for a way to help their daughter—would end up being just up the street nearly 30 years after I'd last read them?

That afternoon, my mom dropped the box on my doorstep, and we wheeled it up to Anna's house in a wagon. Through her glass door, she promised she'd take good care of them and return them to us when she was done. "Enjoy them," I said, knowing that these well-loved books with 30-year-old bindings may not make it through another dog-earing season of childhood love. "They're meant to be read!" If I had ever wondered if I'd be sad to see the books go, I now had my answer: my heart was full of joy watching her haul the books into their living room.

True to her word, Anna did return the books, and my daughter Olivia, now the same age Anna had been when the pandemic began, fell in love with the series, going so far as to create a Best Friend Book Club with a buddy up the street. Olivia knows the journey these books have been on, and how they brought light into the lives of three little girls (so far!). She can't wait to find the next friend who needs a reminder of the goodness in the world.

A time to
keep, and a time
to cast away

CLEANING OUT A CLOSET AND A HEART
— By Laurie Davies —

I SMOOTHED MY skirt and deep-breathed my butterflies into submission as I took the stage for my first-ever public speaking event. "You have 7 seconds to get the audience's attention," my mentor had advised earlier.

My boots hammered a loud, quick cadence on the platform. *Have my seven seconds started? Great. They're already sizing up my clanking boots.*

"Good morning, ladies," I said, looking squarely at the front table for eye contact. Some eyes met mine. Others were oddly transfixed on the 60-foot-wide projection screen behind me.

I glanced back.

Boy, did I have their attention.

The screen screamed "HOARDING" with my name plastered underneath, set against a photograph of an unknown hoarder's home.

Hoarding was something I'd never wanted to talk about. I had seen it take a toll on several people in my life, and I wanted those personal memories to remain musty.

While I'd been invited to speak on having the courage to confront difficult interpersonal dynamics, I planned to keep it high-level and safe. But now, with an introductory slide I hadn't prepared catching me a bit off guard, my mind raced: *Did the event team and I talk about hoarding as a topic for the talk? As THE topic for the talk?* I couldn't remember. Was this God's clever way of pushing open an emotional door I'd kept shut?

I needed to regroup, and fast. "God, give me courage where I lack it," I whispered. Finally, I blurted out a single-word sentence.

"Hoarding," I said.

It hung there for what seemed like several seconds while I flung my preplanned intro into a mental trash can and figured out what to say next. "For some of you the subject is a cable show. For others, it's a source of pain, because you've had a front row seat—like me. I wonder if, for others, it's lining the pathways of your home and your mind."

I somehow managed to get back on track. I drew on the memories of self-doubt—had I done enough to help when I saw the owners of the stacks and piles in my own life had a problem?—to encourage the women to bring others' blind spots gently into the light, even when they're afraid. I used my own experience to offer insight into how to guard your heart without allowing it to become hard—how to establish boundaries lined with empathy in order to offer a path away from any dysfunction in a way that prevents further hurt and bitterness.

I made it through the talk.

Making it through the self-talk would be harder.

Some of my own negative talking points had become almost mythical in my mind. I toggled between competing questions: *Why hadn't I intervened sooner, before the hoarding got out of control? Why did I bother to bring it up at all? Could I have done more? Had I done too much in suggesting the need for professional help?* Confusion always seemed to win when I considered any of the ways hoarding had intersected my own life.

> Those who look to
> him for help will be
> radiant with joy; no
> shadow of shame will
> darken their faces.
> —Psalm 34:5 (NLT)

And yet that day when I stood to speak, the slightest seam opened, letting in a hope of light. Something *had* happened when I saw the word HOARDING form a banner over my name. I had spent years running from shame I'd felt over hoarded conditions I hadn't created, the sense of worthlessness that sank deeper every time I wondered if the stuff was more important than me. And right there in front of two hundred and fifty women—when I couldn't run—God invited me to face those fraudulent feelings of shame, failure, and resentment once and for all.

I wanted to talk to God about His timing. I also wanted to stick the whole thing into a pile labeled "later." But now the gates to the past were open, and I couldn't stop the thoughts and feelings flooding through. Cleaning up years of emotions wouldn't be a tidy afternoon project, so I decided to take aim at my material stuff instead. I rushed home, ready to exhume nooks and crannies, because it's easier to clean out a closet than it is to clean out a heart.

A few stacks of papers that I hadn't even noticed (and my husband had graciously refrained from commenting on) were dealt with immediately—every paper filed, scanned, or shredded. Then I got into the hall closet. Stuff was perched and packed onto shelves. Why was it so hard for me to let things go? Like others in my past, I never seemed to be able to tell objectively if I had enough stuff or too much. Normal clutter or early warning signs? A "collection" or a hoard?

I doubled down and decluttered, saving only heirlooms, games, and seasonal décor. The house felt lighter.

Why didn't I?

The nooks and crannies of my heart needed attention too. That morning, I had prayed for courage to get through a talk, but I sensed God giving me the courage to get rid of my self-talk. God was inviting me to shed my shame. He wanted me to be free.

My pulse quickening with possibilities, I decided to reset my views on what it meant to have "stuff." I pored through Scripture to see what it said about possessions. God flipped my understanding of the word on its head. The first book of Peter calls me God's very own possession. "As a result, you can show others the goodness of God, for he called you out of the darkness into his wonderful light" (1 Peter 2:9, NLT).

It was right there on the page: I am His. As a result, I get to show others how good He is. And the places in my own heart where I'd hoarded hard emotions or shame had been getting in the way. "Stuff" can be good, if it belongs to God. It's the things in our mental closets that cause problems when we can't get rid of them—and sometimes, when we're too close to the situation to know when to let go, we need God to stage an intervention.

At the right time, when God knew I was ready, He invited me to clean house. He led me from darkness into His wonderful light.

A stage in front of hundreds of women is a tough time to punt, which makes it the perfect time for an epiphany.

With the same precision I'd gotten rid of the accumulated stuff in my house, God prompted me to get rid of the accumulated stuff in my heart—including resentment connected to the word *hoarding*. It started that morning when I'd said a hard word out loud, and it continued through a process of counseling when I said harder words out loud.

One by one, I cut loose the chains of shame, regret, and worthlessness I'd been carrying, until one day, I realized my heart and my hands were free. To worship. To serve. To cling to what is good and accept that to God, I am a possession of great value.

I'll be honest, it's still disorienting. I got used to those chains. They were much louder than the quick, sharp cadence of boots clanking across a stage. They were far heavier than all the stuff stacked in my closets.

And yet they pale in power compared to the One who forms a banner over my name.

CHAPTER
6

SPEAKING UP AND BUILDING BRIDGES

ECCLESIASTES 3:7

A time to rend,
and a time to sew;
a time to keep silence,
and a time to speak

INTRODUCTION

Stories of things torn apart and sewn back together,
and of words that came at just the right time

— By Shirley Raye Redmond —

IMAGINE THAT YOU are attending a worship service in Philadelphia—the City of Brotherly Love. You slip from the pew to kneel in fervent prayer. Suddenly, you are interrupted by a firm hand shaking your shoulder. A church deacon hisses, "Get up. You can't sit here." You ask politely if you might be permitted to finish praying and are told that if you do not leave immediately, you will be forcibly escorted from the pew.

That actually happened to Richard Allen (1760–1831), a former enslaved person and respected Methodist preacher. The incident prompted him to establish a congregation where Black people could worship freely and with dignity.

From the moment Richard first heard the gospel at a Methodist revival and accepted Christ at the age of 17, he couldn't stop speaking about the Lord to the other enslaved people on the Delaware plantation where he lived. He even taught himself to read the Bible. He preached the Word so powerfully that eventually his enslaver converted to the Christian faith, offering Richard the opportunity to purchase his freedom. Soon after, Richard became a circuit rider, speaking in Methodist churches throughout Delaware and other nearby states. His powerful preaching and religious fervor impressed prominent White church leaders, who provided him with many opportunities to preach the Word.

Richard eventually moved to Philadelphia, where he attended the St. George's Methodist Church. His leadership at prayer meetings attracted dozens of Black people—all of whom were required to sit along the wall in the "African Corner." When racial tensions increased, Richard realized that his people needed a place where they could worship freely and with dignity. He and his associate Absalom Jones purchased a large building that became the home of the Bethel African Methodist Episcopal Church (AME) in 1793. The congregation grew rapidly.

For more than a decade, the city's Methodist church leaders tried to keep Richard's growing congregation under their authority. Finally, the AME—which had expanded to include leaders in Delaware and New Jersey as well as Pennsylvania—broke away and became an independent denomination in 1816.

Over the years Richard Allen continued to speak out—he preached the gospel; he promoted abolition; he advocated for education for Black people. He and his wife, Sarah, operated a station on the Underground Railroad.

Richard took every opportunity to speak the truth. It should come as no surprise that he became America's first "megachurch" pastor when his budding family of churches had grown to more than seven thousand souls by the early 1820s. Today there are approximately six thousand AME congregations with over 2 million members.

RICHARD ALLEN EXEMPLIFIES Ephesians 4:15 (NIV): "Speaking the truth in love, we will grow to become in every respect the mature body of him who is the head, that is, Christ." In this next chapter, you'll find stories of relationships torn apart and others mended, occasions when people spoke the truth in love like Richard Allen, and other times when silence did indeed prove to be golden.

A time to
rend, and a
time to sew

THE EASTER PARADE

— By Roberta Messner —

OH, NO! SHE can't *be coming to* my *school!*

Teresa, who always knew the scoop, had just stopped by my locker at West Junior High that spring morning in 1966 to fill me in. "We're getting a new history teacher, Roberta," she whispered. "A Mrs. Toole. She's transferring from a school across town." Breathless, Teresa took off for Sandy's locker, a classmate on a mission.

Teresa was always on a mission. The week before, she'd taunted me in front of our entire gym class. "That lady you call 'Mamaw' isn't your *real* grandmother, Roberta. You just *think* she is." I still felt the shame of her mocking voice. Everything I'd always believed about my family had unraveled in those two sentences.

When anything would upset me, I'd always talk to Mamaw about it over one of our sewing projects. But I sure couldn't tell her I'd heard she wasn't my biological grandmother—how a girl at school said when my mamaw married my papaw, he already had kids from when he was married before. Try as I might, I couldn't get Mother to answer my questions. What did all this mean? I loved Mamaw more than anything, but if what they said was true, how was I supposed to even treat her? That evening, as I trailed behind Mother toward our pew at the midweek prayer service, I was still reeling from the news. "Who *am* I anyway?" I wailed. "Am I still a *Baptist*?"

The teacher with the name "Mrs. Toole" meant nothing to Teresa or any of the others. But to me, it meant everything. Everything I now dreaded. By lunch the guys were already cracking jokes. "I bet she has a tool belt around her middle," one of them said. "She'll probably call class to order with a hammer."

Mrs. Toole was one of my grandmother's sewing customers. Mamaw ran an alteration shop out of her little stone cottage, four doors up from my junior high. For special customers like Mrs. Toole, she also created garments from tissue-paper patterns they brought her. For years Mrs. Toole had come calling to Mamaw's, armed with wildly unpredictable fabrics that she'd bought on one of her trips to far-off lands. Most recently she'd brought "a real humdinger," Papaw told me with a whistle and a shake of his head.

Mamaw's kitchen was just off the dining room that doubled as her alteration shop. While I was having a glass of milk at the kitchen table, she filled me in on Mrs. Toole's latest textile. "Wait till you see it, Roberta," she said as she pressed a seam on the ironing board parked by the stove. "It's bright, and I do mean bright." She pushed her wire-rimmed eyeglasses up on her nose. "It's not actually fabric," she said, fingering her worn calico housedress. "It's a tablecloth from India. Judging from the size, I'd say it's a banquet model. But talk about purty!" I nodded and smiled, but my insides were churning. I hadn't seen Mamaw since Teresa had told me about everything. She looked like the same Mamaw I'd loved since forever. But was she? I didn't know what to think or feel.

Regardless of the fabric, Mrs. Toole always requested that her global finds be made into the same boring suit. Simplicity pattern #6685. I could have drawn it in my sleep. It featured a long-sleeved jacket that hit just below the waist and had four buttons down the front. The skirt was a below-the-knee A-line.

Mrs. Toole leaned toward what she called a "continental look" in fashion. When she flew to Japan, she brought back expensive

I am reminded of
your sincere faith,
which first lived in
your grandmother.
−2 Timothy 1:5 (NIV)

seafoam-green silk. She came home with a fanciful embroidered blanket from Pakistan. A tapestry from France. She once had Mamaw sew a long, flowing scarf from a sarong she found in Africa. She selected fine linen in Ireland, tartan plaid in Scotland, and once requested a suit be made from a Persian rug. Mamaw had to buy special heavy-duty machine needles for that one!

"The culture of our world is woven into each country's textiles," I'd heard Mrs. Toole pontificate to Mamaw, her voice rising at least an octave in excitement. She'd go on about how she always gave each student a small square swatch she'd trimmed with just-sharpened pinking shears. Afterward she'd show the class slides of where she discovered the amazing textile.

I was always thrilled that *I* wasn't one of her students. It was bad enough that Mamaw assigned me (with Mrs. Toole's blessing), the task of crafting the bound buttonholes and installing the of-the-moment invisible zippers she preferred . . . "touches only the finest garments possess."

The following Monday morning found me in history class with Mrs. Toole (a.k.a. "6685") at the blackboard. Short and stout like Mamaw's white enamel teapot, she was dressed in one of her all-too-familiar suits. The fabric was none other than the colorful cotton tablecloth from India that had huge golden pears splashed all over a grassy-green background.

I found my seat in the middle row, three desks back. When the guys rolled in, I heard one of them say, "Well, she didn't have to wear the whole pear tree!" Some of the kids laughed right out loud. Others stifled giggles. I felt sick to my stomach thinking of what could happen next.

After she settled the class down, a gray-haired Mrs. Toole sashayed up and down the aisles modeling Mamaw's handiwork and telling all about her travel to India. When she strolled past my desk, I could hear the swish of her green taffeta lining.

My world stopped. "Oh, class," she cooed. "I recognize *this* student. She's the granddaughter of the lady who designs my wardrobe." *She doesn't know the truth about Mamaw,* I agonized. *What if Teresa blurts it out to the whole class?* Willing Teresa to keep quiet, I slumped down in my seat. Mrs. Toole smiled at me and added: "This young lady right here installed the invisible zipper in my skirt." She raised her jacket to give everyone a look-see, then added, "It looks like an ordinary seam. Let's give Roberta a hand for a splendid job."

After class I passed clusters of students, all speculating about this most unusual teacher who "wanted to make history come alive." I caught snatches of my name and laughter about how I'd helped to create her one-of-a-kind costume. Just when I thought things couldn't get worse, they did.

At glee club that afternoon, we practiced the tunes we were to perform in the Easter concert. I was to stand on the front row and sing the opening lines of Irving Berlin's "The Easter Parade" as a solo. As class ended, our glee club teacher announced that after school the following day we would have a dress rehearsal. "Wear your best Easter frocks," she said. I owned no best clothes. I had shot up in height, and all my spring dresses were way too short, even for the sixties.

That evening I told Mother about the upcoming dress rehearsal. She pointed to a zipped bag hanging from the doorframe in our living room. It looked exactly like what Mamaw used to protect garments she worked on for customers.

"Your grandmother dropped this by on her way home from the grocery store," Mother explained. Things were starting to look up. Maybe Mamaw had made me one of the new empire-waisted dresses the girls wore in *Seventeen* magazine. Or sewn me a tent dress with a pleat in the front. I'd seen a Butterick pattern for that. But when Mother unzipped the bag, I nearly died. Inside was a miniature version of Mrs. Toole's pear-patterned suit. "Your mamaw made it for you to wear to the concert," she said to my gasping mouth. "She sewed it from extra fabric she had on hand."

> God sets the
> lonely in families.
> —Psalm 68:6 (NIV)
>
> ∼

Mother had to be kidding! I'd never be caught dead in that thing.

She tried to tell me how Mamaw had spent most of her life on that farm around dreary earthy colors. How this was the cheeriest fabric she'd ever laid her eyes on. "Your grandmother only had 10 dollars to spend on groceries today," Mother said. "But she still bought a can of those Del Monte pears you like and a tub of cottage cheese. She thought this outfit would remind you of your favorite treat."

But Mother's words couldn't penetrate my mortification. The only thing I could do was pray like we did at church. Pray the concert would be canceled. That I'd come down with a virus. That something—anything—would happen so I wouldn't have to wear those pears.

My prayers weren't answered. Come Friday evening, there I was at the concert, bedecked in a pear-studded suit. Some of the kids snickered, but the oddest something came over me, and all of a sudden, it didn't matter. When I looked out into the audience, I spotted Mamaw on the front row of the school auditorium. My eyes played a trick on me. Instead of the familiar figure sitting with the other family members, I saw her bent over her old Singer treadle in the tiny back bedroom that housed her machine. Trying to earn a little extra money to spend on everyone but herself. To give me a gift with a story behind it. Part of her heart too. She loved me enough to give me the bright, beautiful fabric that she'd wished she could wear herself, and that love—that made us family. Love mattered more than blood.

When I began my solo, Teresa's taunts were the furthest thing from my mind:

In your Easter bonnet, with all the frills upon it,
You'll be the grandest lady in the Easter parade . . .

Funny thing was, I *felt* like the grandest lady. Especially when Mamaw flashed that beaming smile of hers. *My mamaw*, family through and through. The mamaw I'd choose out of every mamaw in the world.

A time to
rend, and a
time to sew

ZAPPED OUT OF THE HOLE

— By Kelly J. Stigliano —

"HELLO?" I ANSWERED the phone and jumped at the deafening response from the other end.

"You won't believe what I found," she wailed. "I saw our cell phone bill lying on the kitchen table. It had page after page of calls from Douglas to that tramp. I confronted him, and he said the calls were all business related. Sixty calls each day, Kelly!"

"Now Franny, just wait a minute," I tried to be calm. "Let's not jump to conclusions. Douglas loves you. Let's talk about this."

"I'll be over later," she promised.

When I had met Francis 5 years earlier, we had a lot in common. I was the wife of the newest guy on staff at a small company. My husband was their local representative. Her husband was the assistant manager. We were both Christians. We were both silly and slightly irreverent. I came from Ohio. She and her husband, Douglas, had moved to northern Florida from Ireland with their sons 3 years before.

Being the new girl in town, I needed to know where to buy fresh vegetables, who the favorite veterinarian was, and which medical practice to call our own. Francis was there for every decision I had to make. As we both faced a new life in a place that was very different from where we'd grown up, we formed a bond that quickly grew, and we became the best of friends.

In time, the manager retired, and Douglas took his position. Although he had been a great assistant, Douglas's administrative skills were weak, and things became lax in the office. Francis complained about her husband's lack of initiative with his staff.

Then it happened. Douglas was smitten by a beautiful southern belle named Dreama, who walked into his office asking for a job yet undefined—that of inventory specialist. He hired her, and in short time, she began to seek his counsel for problems she was having with her husband. Her tearful evening visits to Douglas's office turned heads. He insisted that nothing personal was going on. However, Dreama soon left her husband and seemed to have a hold on her boss.

At two o'clock that afternoon, Francis banged on my door. I opened it, and she rushed in, knocking my shoulder as she pushed past me. Her face was red from hours of crying.

"You've got to see this," she howled.

I put the water on for tea while she frantically searched her large handbag. She dumped the contents onto the floor and rifled through the pile, but there was no sign of the bill she'd mentioned in her earlier call. Grabbing her cell phone, my dear friend muttered curses as she punched the numbers with determination.

Her face turned a deeper shade of red. She faced the phone and screamed, her Irish accent so heavy that I could hardly understand her as she demanded that Douglas tell her where he put the phone bill.

She threw her cell phone across the room. She was hoarse from screaming. Her husband had taken the phone bill, never to have it appear again. Further, during the call he'd accused her of losing the bill.

After that, Francis and I talked daily as he worked overtime trying to convince everyone—from the organization's leaders to the cleaning lady—that Francis's accusations of infidelity were a result of insane jealousy.

Isolated, she became more and more dependent on me. I attempted damage control. With her naturally dramatic personality, she seemed to enjoy the crisis, and her behavior became more erratic.

"Francis, you have to stop calling everyone and making scenes," I admonished after she was arrested for an aggressive confrontation. "You're just proving Douglas right!"

I gave her information on how to deal with a cheating spouse. I did the investigative computer work and counseling, and Francis did the midnight sleuthing—visiting hotel rooms and sneaking around Dreama's house.

Over the next year I went with her to an attorney, suggested counselors, and listened endlessly. It was a slippery slope, and I went down fast.

Initially I tried to keep Francis calm and help her take the right steps to recover her marriage and reputation. But eventually I found myself saying, "Throw his junk out onto the lawn and hope it rains!" That certainly did not help.

One day I read another long email from my troubled friend about Douglas and Dreama. Franny had found romantic greeting cards in the trash can when she broke into his office in the middle of the night. I closed the email, sat back in my chair, and sighed.

My Bible reading that morning had included Philippians 4, and verse 8 echoed in my mind: "Whatever is true, whatever is honorable, whatever is just, whatever is pure, whatever is lovely, whatever is commendable, if there is any excellence, if there is anything worthy of praise, think about these things" (ESV).

My phone rang.

As I laid my hand on the receiver, I paused. *I'm not happy*, I silently prayed. *I feel so yucky. This is going nowhere. Help me, Lord.*

That one quick prayer was like a zap of electricity that infused me with clarity, strength, and boldness.

"Oh, hi, Francis. Yes, I got your email," I said. Then, I heard my voice say with courage, "No, I'm not going to answer you. You are choosing to not change or do anything about Douglas's actions. I don't want to talk about Douglas and Dreama anymore. There are so many other things we can talk about. If you want to talk about more positive things, I'd love to still be your friend. Negativity is contagious, and it isn't healthy, Franny. It isn't healthy for you *or* me. I've got to be more positive."

She hung up on me. I was shaking. I leaned back and took a deep breath. "Thank You, Lord."

While my heart hurt for what I suspected was a lost friendship, I felt relief. Clearly it had been the time to uproot the decaying weed of cynicism in my life.

Francis seemed quite comfortable residing in her dramatic hole of despair, and I had allowed myself to crawl in with her and be enveloped with hatred and bitterness. It was time to leave. Within a week, Francis found someone else to take my place as her sounding board.

> If I speak in the tongues of men and of angels, but have not love, I am a noisy gong or a clanging cymbal.
> –1 Corinthians 13:1 (ESV)

Moving forward, I resolved to plant positivity. While concentrating on the love of my family, my spiritual growth, and my creativity, the Lord opened doors I couldn't have imagined.

Within the first year post-Francis, I discovered the thrill of being published, and my calendar filled with speaking opportunities.

Eliminating the dark, ugly negativity from my life and thinking on what was lovely and worthy of praise enabled me to share positive lessons to audiences throughout the southeastern United States.

I'm learning that there is a time to be silent and a time to speak. By speaking my frustration—first to God and then to my friend—I was able to rid myself of a toxic relationship and open myself up to the paths He wanted me to follow. I used the power of my words to share what I'd learned with others and encourage and uplift them. My supreme Guide showed me the way to be exactly where I needed to be.

LESSONS FROM AN EMPTY FUEL TANK

— By Glenda Ferguson —

OH, NO! WHY did SHE have to park her van right next to me?

This was not the time I wanted to dwell on hurt feelings about something that happened between us a year earlier.

I was at a small country church, 20 minutes outside town, to mourn the unexpected loss of our beloved school secretary. So many of us teachers were attending the funeral that we were asked to parallel park our vehicles off the narrow road, opposite the cemetery. My compact car was pointed downhill toward the woods, with both front tires sliding off the pavement. Parking right alongside me was Tina.

Since Tina was still in her driver's seat, I wanted to time my exit from my car so I didn't meet up with her. I thought I had let go of the animosity between us, but suddenly, my stress and bitter memories of what had happened with her son last year assaulted me. Her son had been in my class at school. When he'd gotten in trouble at recess, the recess teacher had sent him directly to the principal, who suspended him for a day. The students had already been talking about it when they came back from recess, but Tina had blamed me, thinking that I had broadcast his wrongdoing to the class. She sent emails to both me and the principal, complaining about what she believed I had done. We never confronted one another, let alone resolved the issue. In fact, I thought I had taken the high road by not gossiping to my colleagues about the matter. I had prayed that God would resolve the situation.

But, just now, I realized I was still holding a grudge.

Not able to delay any longer, I got out of the car and walked across the road, hoping to blend in with a group. Yet there she was. Both of us walking toward the church at the same time. We nodded to one another.

I entered the church, greeted the family, and sat in a crowded pew waiting for the service. I overheard Rita, a fellow teacher, ask Tina if she wanted to squeeze in. Tina said, "I'm just here to give the family my condolences; then I have to leave early to go to work."

I felt a bit of relief and forgot all about her.

But a few minutes later Tina showed up at the pew again. Tina told Rita, "My van is out of gas. I thought I had enough to get from home to the church then to the gas station. But I guess the way the van is parked downhill, there's not enough to back out."

I stifled a laugh and sarcastic comment.

Rita started asking others in our pew about helping Tina. I avoided eye contact while one person after another said they had prior commitments and couldn't help her. Rita said, "I would help you out, but I told the family I would serve at the dinner afterward." Then she turned to me, "Glenda, what about you?"

All eyes were on me, even Tina's. I gazed into Rita's eyes attempting to communicate, "No, not me!" However, I found myself saying, "If Tina can wait till after the graveside service . . ."

"Yes," Tina quickly said.

All through the church service, I regretted my offer. On the inside, my heart was still full of anger toward Tina. During the service, I felt a twinge of guilt when the minister told everyone how our school secretary had demonstrated such a giving heart by helping others.

Slowly I walked with the others toward the cemetery. I was still mumbling to myself, but mostly to God. Why was it me helping her, and why now? I offered up a prayer for guidance in assisting Tina with a friendly attitude.

I trudged toward my car, where Tina was waiting.

"Ready to go?" I said as I got in.

She said, "I don't have a gas can. I'll have to buy one at the gas station."

That's just perfect. So much for my friendly attitude.

As I backed my car out, I stepped on the gas to get my front tires over the pavement.

Tina said, "That was my trouble. There was enough gas to get the van started, but it died. The little bit of gas I had shifted around when I tried to get my wheels up and over the pavement."

We managed to share some small talk on the drive to town. But I did feel a nudge from deep inside. I was curious and asked, "Is your son having a better year this year than he did last year?"

Tina looked at me and said, "Not really." Tina mentioned how much her son enjoyed the routines in my classroom and how he missed me. Her positive comments seemed sincere, which surprised me. Was it possible she had forgotten all about what I thought was a major incident?

Tina directed me to the nearest gas station, but they had no gas cans. So I drove to another station. She purchased a red plastic container with a safety spout and filled it at the gas pump.

During the drive back to the church, Tina continued talking about school and her son's classroom. She never mentioned his wrongdoing

> I ask you to forgive your brothers the sins and the wrongs they committed in treating you so badly.
>
> —Genesis 50:17 (NIV)

in my room, and neither did I. Why had I allowed that burden to occupy my mind so long? I just wanted to let go of the anger.

After almost an hour, we were back at the church. That's when both of us encountered frustration. During the trip, gasoline had spilled into my trunk, leaving noxious fumes. I grabbed napkins out of my glove compartment to mop up the spill. Then neither one of us knew how to operate the safety spout so we could pour gasoline directly into the tank of Tina's van. Gasoline splashed onto my high heels and onto Tina's work uniform. I grabbed more napkins. We didn't know whether to laugh or laugh some more. Finally she salvaged a gallon in the tank.

I knew I had missed out on the fellowship at the dinner. So I said, "Tina, I'm going to follow you until you get close to your work, just to make sure you have enough gas."

I thought she might become stranded, and this time, I was sincere about my offer.

Tina said, "You don't have to do that. But I do appreciate your help. I have learned my lesson. From now on, I am going to make sure my tank has gas." This time all went well when she started her van and backed out.

God used an empty gas tank to teach me a lesson, too, about reconciling with others quickly. When I was finally alone in my car, following behind Tina, I could smell the gasoline fumes from my shoes and the trunk, but I knew they would dissipate over time, just like my anger had today.

If our encounter had been right after her email, I would not have had the grace to respond as I did at a later time. It seems that the Lord allows our feelings to simmer for a while. Only He knows over the passage of time when we will be ready to do what He wished all along—reconcile.

NOT IF YOU'RE A WOMAN PREACHER

— By Jeanette Levellie —

"THIS IS ONE OF the hardest emails I've ever written . . ." I read. *What on earth?* I couldn't imagine why my friend Lucy, the director of a Christian writers' conference where I'd spoken several times, would say this to me. *Have I done something to offend her and she's axing me from her list of class presenters?*

In the most diplomatic terms, Lucy informed me that the conference's board of directors had recently made a new rule. In the future, they would not allow any woman who was an ordained minister to teach a class or give a message to the general assembly. They believed that God only meant men to preach.

I stared at the screen in shock, my pulse pounding in my temples. I may or may not have blinked to keep unshed tears from spilling down my face.

Over the previous decade, I'd spoken at Lucy's conference four times. I'd presented six different classes, given three morning messages, and met with dozens of attendees, advising them on how to publish their writing. Many of those people, including Lucy, had become dear friends. Due to the absence of awards and posturing I'd seen at other conferences, I'd always told Lucy that this conference was my idea of "a preview of heaven." There were no cliques, no pecking order, and everyone was welcomed. Up to now.

Why would the conference directors suddenly change their minds about the suitability of women speakers, who made up the majority of their teachers? My love for the Lord and commitment to Him hadn't changed. My talent as a speaker hadn't diminished. I hoped it had blossomed and grown. Even my title hadn't changed. I didn't choose to use Rev. before my name. So I went from Jeanette Levellie, Author and Speaker, to Jeanette Levellie, Author and Speaker. And how did the board even know my status had changed?

Perhaps they'd come across a biography in one of the anthologies I wrote for, sharing how I'd become ordained—a milestone I was especially pleased about and thankful for. The thought had never occurred to me that my calling to preach God's Word would exclude me from teaching classes on the art of writing. Or giving a morning message titled "How Sweet It Is" about the joys of the writing life. The audience loved catching the candy I threw out during that "sermon."

Even my husband, Kevin, who'd been an ordained minister and pastor for the previous 45 years, applauded my decision and supported me in this new venture. *If it doesn't offend Kevin that God has called me to preach, why should these people veto it?* I was confused, shocked, and sad. But not angry. That lack of resentment surprised me almost as much as Lucy's announcement.

Since I was a small child, people had teased me about the relationship between my red hair and my quick temper. I always denied the silly wives' tale. But God—and my husband—knew how much I struggled to overcome my low boiling point. There was a time when receiving an email like this would've sparked an angry email in response as I pounded indignant words on the page, and an hour later I'd be crying in my husband's arms at my lack of self-control. It was the issue I'd prayed about continually over the last four decades. The issue I worked on the most, reading self-help books and memorizing Bible verses about love. The issue I wondered if I'd ever master.

Was God showing me that all those prayers and hard work hadn't been in vain? I marveled at the lack of anger in my heart. I'd noticed several times in the last couple of

> See, I have placed before you an open door that no one can shut.
> —Revelation 3:8 (NIV)

years that my temper over minor annoyances didn't flare up as often as before. But this email from Lucy was a major assault of rejection from dear friends. Like the flash of orange when a fire ignites, the miracle of my changed heart hit me. My tears of sorrow suddenly changed to tears of joy at this miraculous breakthrough.

Before responding to Lucy's email, I knew I needed to pray for wisdom. I wanted to show Lucy that I didn't blame her for something that was out of her hands. I actually felt sorry for her. From the tone of her email, I sensed that she didn't necessarily agree with the board's stance. She even told me I was one of her favorite people in the world. That made me smile. "Help me, Jesus"—my favorite prayer— was the best one I could whisper in my dazed state of mind.

I phrased my email to Lucy as graciously as I could manage, but still shared my feelings. "I'm certainly not mad, just disappointed and very, very sad." Lucy wrote back agreeing with me that it was a matter of semantics—their interpretation of Scripture vs. mine— and told me she was super sorry to lose me as a faculty member.

Later, I would work to avoid any trace of bitterness when I broke the news to my close friends Kate and Rocky, fellow speakers at the conference. The three of us traveled together to save on expenses.

Kate and Rocky's reactions didn't surprise me. Both withdrew their names from consideration as future faculty for the conference. I was, however, astounded that Rocky took the time to write a passionate email to the board of directors, asking them to reconsider their decision. I wondered if he knew his letter wouldn't do any good. Or if he just needed to get the disappointment and anger off his chest. Of course, the people in charge of the conference didn't change their minds. But my friends' loyalty would help ease the pain in my broken heart.

On the day I got the news, though, I was still trying to figure out what to do. "Okay, God, now what? Regardless of how I feel about the fairness of the board's decision, that door has closed. Please help me to handle this in a mature way."

That same afternoon my boss—the pastor of the church where I serve as administrative assistant—approached me. "We need a preacher to fill the pulpit for the Sunday I'm gone next month. Are you interested?" Although my heart hadn't yet recovered from the shock of Lucy's email and the loss it meant, I didn't hesitate to tell my boss that I'd be overjoyed to preach.

The following day, another conference director emailed me to ask if I could teach a class at their conference next spring. Good ol' Rocky, who'd taught classes for them in the past, had recommended me. By the time the Zoom meeting with the conference directors ended, they'd put me down for three classes. New avenues of ministry were before my eyes.

Although these new opportunities didn't erase the sadness I felt over being uninvited to my favorite conference, they helped. A lot. The elation I experienced at God's hand moving so quickly shocked me almost as much as the email from Lucy. In my experience as a Christian, God usually takes a lot longer than I like to fix problems. When people tell me, "God is never late," I want to say, "Yes, but does He have to wait till the last minute?"

It appeared that when the door to ministry at the writers' conference closed, God looked down, saw my dilemma, and opened a couple of new doors. He knew before I received this hurtful blow that it would happen. Because He's timeless, God had already mapped out the solution.

I once heard a preacher say that God doesn't cause tragedies or disappointments, but instead He weaves them into the tapestry of His plan. God didn't cause the decision that led to my heartbreak. But He gave me the grace to forgive and move on.

That grace was the real miracle in this story. Not the perfect timing of new opportunities zinging my way. Not even the heartening support of my friends. But the miracle of a soft heart that kept me from bitterness. Only God can do that.

A time to keep
silence, and
a time to speak

WHERE THE SIDEWALK BEGINS

— By Ashley Kappel —

HISTORIC NEIGHBORHOOD STREETS are great for many
things: homes are closer together for visiting with neighbors, little town
centers are just around the corner, and almost any holiday turns into a
yard-friendly block party teeming with kids. But those same 18-foot-
wide streets, built long before I was born, can be pretty treacherous for
sharing space with bikes, scooters, and friend-seeking elementary
students heading to school, the neighborhood pool, or the library.

When we moved in, I noticed that there were no sidewalks in
our neighborhood. *How could this be*, I thought. *There are two hundred
kids from these few streets that walk to our school each morning!*

That evening, I gathered my two toddlers and headed to our
city council meeting, where I showed pictures of the narrow street
and asked how to go about getting sidewalks. "Check with your
neighbors and come back to us," they said. "We've got the funding
here; we just need the goodwill."

Thrilled, I headed home, typed up a quick note ("Great News!"),
and dropped it off at a few dozen homes around ours. But then, the
calls started. I had included my contact information in case people
wanted to help. How naïve I was!

*These roads aren't designed for sidewalks. I'll lose my whole yard!
We've lived without them for 50 years here; you can do the same.* Over

and over the messages rolled in, each breaking my heart. How can sidewalks, something to connect our citizens to each other and our local resources, be divisive? *Lord, help me see,* I prayed. *And tell me what to say!*

I returned to the city council the next week, tail between my legs but also armed with video of cars speeding down our street, SUVs running stop signs, and photos showing what I thought could be done to counter the objections we'd received. While we discussed the neighbors' responses, my toddlers ran through the meeting room eating all the snacks I had packed.

Following that second meeting, little by little I gained traction. Neighbors who were thrilled started to reach out. "Finally, a way for the kids to move around without us worrying so," one texted me. I walked our street with each councilman during the day, when streets were quiet, and still they were in awe of how busy our road was, and how impossible it was to get out of the way when you needed to. Still, I prayed for patience, now knowing that I was facing a battle—and a very uphill one, both literally given the slope of the road and figuratively within the community.

How right I was! What I thought would be a quick project, at least on my part, turned into an 18-month slog. During that time, the council met with each homeowner to discuss where the sidewalk would fall on their property, negotiated a few tree removals, and went through about a dozen iterations of what the sidewalk would look like once complete. I also had another child during those 18 months, joking at the biweekly meetings that I had created a human in the time we had argued over half a mile of concrete.

I played nice, said the right things, and showed up every other Monday night without fail. While sometimes I wanted to speak up and move people toward a faster resolution, I knew that pushing for too much, too fast might get the whole project shelved. But I also cheered

> The Lord is not slow in keeping his promise, as some understand slowness.
>
> —2 Peter 3:9 (NIV)

～

on the inside when I realized I now came with a whole troop of neighbors, all campaigning for what we considered a community improvement. *I feel like I'm doing what I'm supposed to,* I prayed. *Help me to continue doing the right thing and wait on Your perfect timing.*

That next week, a dad showed up at the meeting who had been many times before. After the meeting opened and we again discussed the plans, which were now drawn up, budget-approved, and street-ready, the dad stood up. "I need to say something. Is it not time? You have met with every family whose yard will be impacted. You have accommodated every wish for saving trees and keeping yards. We have gone through the start of two more school years without having a way to walk safely. These families have come week after week and listened and been patient. What else do you need? It's time." Finally, someone said what we were all thinking!

The council dismissed that night, and, since the plans were already approved, made the announcement on our city website that the work would begin immediately. I could hardly believe it!

As expected, the construction took almost no time. Within a few weeks, the path was laid out, the concrete was poured, and the sidewalks were there. The city worked hard to accommodate neighbors' requests, so now we happily boast that we have the curviest sidewalks in the state, but I don't mind. I'll take a safe, curvy path to a friend's house any day of the week.

We've had the sidewalks several years now. That sweet baby that was born during the process is now four, and loves running down them to see his friend five houses down. My husband and I walk them every morning as we finish our morning loop. And I can look out my front window and see that I made a difference to better my community.

Thankfully, I also know enough to look inward and see what the process of getting our sidewalks did to improve me. If everything had worked out my way and the sidewalks had appeared instantly, I never would have learned the lessons I feel God needed me to understand about how to navigate difficult relationships in my own backyard. I also wouldn't have forged such strong friendships with the neighbors who did feel the need for what I considered a neighborhood improvement. Throughout this process, I learned that even if I'm going about everything the "right" way, I still need to wait for the plan to unfold in God's perfect time.

A time to keep
silence, and a
time to speak

THE WRONG PERSON TO MARRY

— By Rhoda Blecker —

BARBARA'S VOICE ON the phone was filled with excitement. "I'm getting married again—at last," she said. "We'll be in Los Angeles next week, and I want you and Keith to meet him!"

Since we had first met, Barbara and I had shared our lives in a long series of phone calls, even when we'd both lived in LA. In addition to telling each other everything about what was going on with ourselves, we talked about Judaism (she was from a much more observant background than I was), books, scholarship, dating, current events, our work, our interests—everything that mattered or that made us who we were. And we found something funny in all of it, especially in the inexplicable absurdity of so much God seemed to have built into life. We laughed with each other in every call.

The phone calls during her contentious divorce were heavier, and yet I would try to find ways to make us laugh. The call where I simply couldn't do that was the one where her voice was angry, but very tightly controlled: "He's going to fight to deny me custody if I don't sell the house," she said. I knew their house had been hers before the wedding, and that she loved it, but clearly the children were more important. There was nothing absurd or funny about the situation. After that call, I began to pray for Barbara to be happy again.

Once the house was sold, Barbara and the kids moved several thousand miles away, a challenging journey for which she packed and drove a full-size moving van (and, no, she did not have a trucker's license) to a tiny apartment on the campus of the university at which she would go on to get a PhD, while raising her family as a single mother. Her first phone call to me from her new "home" began, "If I could do that, I can do *anything*!" We laughed quite a bit at her adventures in moving.

Over the next almost a decade, as she finished her studies, got her degree, found an assistant professorship at a prestigious eastern university, and moved again, there were more phone calls with laughter. But I also sensed strongly that Barbara was tired of being the only one doing everything, making all the decisions, being alone. My prayer for her became, "Please notice that Barbara needs a better husband."

So when I got her phone call about what seemed to be the answer to that prayer, I was thrilled. We made a lunch date for a nice place in Beverly Hills, and Keith and I met the prospective groom. Several hours later, my husband and I went back to our apartment. We wouldn't be going to the wedding, which was scheduled for 5 months in the future back on the East Coast.

I thought about what the lunch date had shown me—twice, Barbara's fiancé had started to tell stories about her. She asked him not to. He went ahead anyway, disregarding what she wanted. In fact, he ignored her throughout the lunch, keeping his attention focused on us—and trying to keep our attention focused on him. "If he's behaving like that *before* they're married, how is he going to act afterward?" I asked Keith.

Later that evening, the phone rang, and Barbara asked, "How did you like him?"

I'd been debating all afternoon what to say when she asked me that question, as I knew she would. I'd asked her about Keith before

> Jonathan, out of
> his love for David,
> adjured him . . .
> –1 Samuel 20:17 (JPS)
>
> ～

we got married, and she had reinforced every good thing I believed about him, which had filled me with joy. I wanted her to have that feeling too. And in Judaism, we are directed to tell a bride that she is beautiful on her wedding day whether we think it's true or not. We are always supposed to be aware of other people's feelings and to be kind, even if it stretches the truth.

And yet . . .

There had always been truth between Barbara and me, even when the truth wasn't funny. We would mostly find ways to bring out the absurdity in it and laugh together. I knew very well how much Barbara did not want to be alone any longer. I was convinced the kind thing to do was to say I liked him. But when I answered her, what came out was, "Barbara, I didn't like the way he was treating you. He wasn't paying attention to what you wanted."

She was silent for so long that I guessed that answer was the last thing she expected, and she ended the call abruptly. I second-guessed myself all evening. Had I hurt her? Would her marriage unavoidably weaken our friendship?

As the date of the wedding drew closer and Barbara hadn't called me to talk about the preparations or personalities of her idiosyncratic family, I grew more and more certain that I should have just kept my opinion to myself. It wasn't unusual for the two of us to go months without speaking, but I was worried that I'd upset her. "Why didn't you warn me?" I asked both Keith and God. Keith gave me the only answer I heard: "Would you have listened to me?"

The evening of the day of the wedding, Barbara called. "I canceled the wedding today," she said.

All I could think of to say was, "Today?"

"Better late than never," she said firmly, then went on to tell me that she had been wearing the wedding dress when she realized she couldn't actually go through with it. The out-of-town guests had found a note on the door of the venue saying there wasn't going to be a wedding after all; the caterer had got paid, but was stuck with a lot of food; her mother was upset, and her kids were delighted. I thought the image of the canceled wedding was the most absurd thing we had ever laughed at, but I was of the same opinion as her kids.

"You were right," she went on. "I kept hearing what you said and noticing it in him, and I didn't want another marriage like the first one."

"And you were right, too," I told her. "You can do anything!"

And I spent the next 5 years thanking God for giving me the strength to be true to myself and to my beloved friend. Then, when she met the wonderful man she finally did marry, I thanked God for solving the problem—even though it would have been better if it had happened a little sooner.

CHAPTER
7

FINDING PEACE

ECCLESIASTES 3:8

A time to love,
and a time to hate;
a time of war,
and a time of peace

INTRODUCTION

Stories of battles won, peace found, and the path to love

— By Shirley Raye Redmond —

JAPANESE DIPLOMAT CHIUNE Sugihara risked his prestigious position and the lives of his wife, Yukiko, and their children in a courageous effort to save thousands of strangers during World War II. Chiune served as the Japanese Empire's vice consul in Lithuania from 1939 to 1940. He had just taken up his responsibilities there when Hitler's army invaded Poland and streams of frantic Jewish refugees flooded Kaunas, Lithuania's temporary capital.

As the news spread about the organized killing of Jews—ordered by Adolf Hitler—the number of refugees increased to staggering numbers. Hundreds of desperate men, women, and children with frightened faces and bloodshot eyes congregated outside Sugihara's consulate. Distraught, Chiune cabled Tokyo to find out what he should do. After all, Imperial Japan and Nazi Germany were allies.

Risking professional disgrace, he issued hundreds of transit visas permitting Jews to flee to the Far East and from there on to Palestine, America, and Canada. Chiune and his wife gave up meals and sleep to produce hundreds, then thousands, of exit visas, each one handwritten, stamped, and numbered. At night, Yukiko massaged her husband's cramped arms and hands. She quit nursing their young son when stress caused her milk to dry up.

When his superiors ordered Chiune to cease issuing visas and to return to Tokyo immediately, he continued to sign as many visas as he could while Yukiko packed their belongings. He told her, "I may have to disobey my government, but if I do not, I will be disobeying God." Once on the train, Chiune handed signed transit visas out the window to the frantic throng crowded on the platform.

After his return to Japan, Chiune was forced to resign from the diplomatic corps in disgrace. He and his family lived in squalor for a time as he tried to earn a living performing menial tasks and selling light bulbs door to door. He occasionally wondered if his sacrifice had done any good at all.

But in 1969, he learned that it had. A young man named Yehosha Nishi came to Japan to thank Chiune for saving his life. With tears running down his cheeks, Nishi showed Chiune a signed transit visa, now worn and yellowed with age. Nishi also shared his testimony with the Yad Vashem in Israel. Soon, hundreds of other grateful "Sugihara Jews" came forward with their own accounts of the former diplomat's self-sacrificing efforts on their behalf.

In 1985 the State of Israel honored Chiune by naming him "Righteous Among the Nations," the only Japanese national to be recognized in this way. Chiune was too ill to attend the ceremony, but his wife and son were there on his behalf and met with Holocaust survivors who'd been saved by Chiune's hastily scribbled exit visas. It is estimated that approximately one hundred thousand people alive today are direct descendants of his rescued refugees.

YOU MAY NEVER be called upon to make a decision that will put your life or job at risk, but like Chiune Sugihara, we all face times of conflict and uncertainty. In this final chapter, you will discover stories of war and peace—relationships torn apart by conflict and then brought back together; people at war with themselves. You'll also find stories of love, with people brought together just in time to live their best lives together. Regardless of the situation or the resolution, God's timing is always perfect.

A time to
love, and a
time to hate

THE MATCHMAKER AND THE COUPON

— By Ellen Fannon —

I SAT ON the beach watching the waves lap at the shoreline, pouring out my broken heart to God. Surrounded by the beauty of His creation, I felt the comfort of His presence envelop me and fill me with His peace, despite what had just happened. A few days earlier, my husband of 13 years left me for another woman. The rest of my life stretched out like an empty, lonely vacuum. We had been together for 17 years, and the prospect of trying to find someone new to share my life with seemed daunting and unappealing. The words flowed softly from my heart.

Father, the idea of spending the rest of my life alone frightens and depresses me. But You know it takes me a long time to get close to people. I would like to get remarried someday, but only if it is in Your will. If remarriage is Your plan for my life, I ask You to direct me to the right man, even though I can't begin to imagine who that might be. Besides, who would want me? I'm a used-up, 36-year-old soon-to-be divorcée.

As I sat there praying, I knew one thing for certain. If remarriage was in my future, this time God would have to be the matchmaker. I had not done so well on my own.

And Father, if remarriage is not Your plan for my life, I ask that You help me be content and fruitful as a single woman. And I also ask that You help me be a better Christian than I have been for the past several years.

I had accepted Christ as a teenager, but I hadn't lived much like a Christian for a long time. I had drifted away from God and desperately wanted the closeness I once had with Him again.

Although I was a member of a local church, I had not attended that particular church in more than 8 years because I had taken a job as the "temporary" organist at a different church. One Sunday night, I felt led to go back to my old church. After the service, I turned around, and there, in the pew behind me, sat a tall, dark-haired man. As we left the sanctuary, a mutual acquaintance introduced me to him—his name was Doug—and we talked for a few minutes in the church foyer. Ordinarily, making small talk with strangers is uncomfortable for me, and, I'm ashamed to admit, I often forget their words as soon as they have spoken. But I vividly remember the curious thought that ran through my mind as I talked with this man: I needed to pay close attention to this conversation, because I would later want to recall every detail. Despite this advice to myself, within a short time, most of what we talked about was a blur. I just remember feeling an instant connection to him. It turned out Doug had just moved to the area, courtesy of the Air Force— although this was the last place he wanted to be. He had come from flying F-16s in Korea to a desk job at Eglin Air Force Base, just as the Persian Gulf War was ramping up. There is nobody more unhappy than a grounded pilot. To add insult to injury, his wife had left him for another man while he was deployed overseas.

I can't explain the immediate bond I felt with this man. It wasn't just our similar sad circumstances. A tinge of disappointment came over me, however, because before we parted, Doug didn't ask for my phone number. I went back to church the following Sunday night, hoping to see him again. But although he did come that night and we talked briefly, he still didn't ask for my number. (I later found out he hadn't been feeling well and had only come to church that

> Take delight in the LORD,
> and he will give you
> your heart's desires.
> —Psalm 37:4 (NLT)

~

night hoping to see me.) Thinking I had read more into his interest than was actually there, I decided to give it one more week. After that, if nothing developed, I was going to stop putting myself in his path.

The third Sunday night, he sat with me. After the service, there was a reception for a missionary couple, and he asked me if I wanted to stay.

"I don't think so," I replied, "I don't know them."

"Let's just stay for a few minutes," he said.

I agreed. The few minutes turned into our being among the last to leave. We were so engrossed in our conversation, we didn't want the evening to end. Still desiring to continue our time together, he suggested we go somewhere for a bite to eat. Unfortunately, nothing was open, so I invited him back to my house. I didn't know it at the time, but God's matchmaking had already been working in both of us. In fact, Doug had driven past my house a couple of times the previous day, hoping to accidentally run into me. He didn't let on that he knew where I lived as he followed me back to the house. We talked until after midnight.

At the end of the evening, Doug mentioned, casually, "I have a coupon for a buy-one-get-one-free dinner at the officer's club that's getting ready to expire. I'd hate to waste it. Would you like to go with me?"

I managed to contain my amused reaction to his odd invitation, while trying to decide whether I should feel flattered or insulted. While not the passionate declaration of desire to spend time in my charming company I might have wished for, nevertheless, it *was* an invitation. I didn't realize it was his awkward attempt to ask me out without making it sound like he was "asking me out." He only admitted that fact to me later. And, although his method left a bit to be desired, it really would have been a shame for that coupon to expire. As a coupon-clipping fanatic myself, I know the pain of missed opportunities for a buy-one-get-one-free deal.

God brought Doug into my life on March 3, 1991, just six short weeks after my prayer. Our first date for the two-for-one dinner took place on March 19. After that night, we were inseparable. On April 6, he asked me to marry him, and I accepted. If anyone had told me I would meet someone, fall in love, and become engaged within 5 weeks, I would have said they were crazy. I am a cautious, practical person who doesn't rush blindly into situations. I seldom even buy things on impulse. Most of my decisions are weighed over time after careful thought. Doug is the same way. But after our first date, I knew with unmistakable clarity this was the man God intended me to spend the rest of my life with. We married on October 5. I never had a doubt. Some people might have thought we moved too fast, but we knew God had brought us together, and there was no reason for us to wait.

It's amazing what can happen when God's hand is at work. Doug and I recently celebrated our thirtieth wedding anniversary. Our 30 years together have been an incredible adventure of discovering the journey God has for us. From Doug retiring as a pilot in the Air Force to a 13-year journey to his becoming a full-time pastor—with many unexpected detours along the way—our lives have been exciting and full of blessings. God led us into a 2-year assignment with the Southern Baptist International Mission Board that took us to the other side of the world and allowed us to return several years later to coordinate disaster relief after the 2004 tsunami. He called us to become foster parents to more than forty children and gave us two adopted sons. We have been blessed to travel all over the world, including two unforgettable trips to the Holy Land.

As clichéd as it may sound, my husband is my other half, my soulmate, my biggest supporter, best friend, and love of my life. We are perfectly attuned to one another and share the same faith, values, and goals. I can truthfully say we have rarely had a disagreement. There is no question that God brought us together at exactly the right time in our lives for each other and for specific work in His Kingdom. Although we sometimes wish we had met earlier in our lives and hadn't gone through the pain of spousal betrayal and divorce, we recognize that the frequent moves Doug made with the military would have conflicted with my career ambitions, making our relationship difficult when we were younger. We also weren't the same people before we met at 36. Our previous, individual experiences taught us valuable lessons on what is truly important—namely, putting God first in everything.

While our divorces left ugly scars, we discovered that God could and would still use us, scars and all. Doug and I sometimes joke about what would have happened to our relationship if that coupon had expired. But I believe the God who brought us together at just the right time could have miraculously intervened to change that expiration date.

A time to
love, and a
time to hate

TWO WEEKS THAT CHANGED MY LIFE

— By Kristen West —

IT WAS A chance encounter that changed the trajectory of my life forever.

I had been a single mother for 10 years. And, if we're being honest, I'd gotten to a place where I was perfectly content to stay that way. I wasn't searching for a husband, and I didn't spend my days sitting at home pining for one, either. My life was full. I was raising two young children on my own, working full-time as a reporter, and using what little time I had left over to foster a few friendships.

During a portion of this season in my life, my children and I shared a home with another single mother and her son. This helpful arrangement gave both of us a built-in babysitter, the grace of sharing the financial load, and some like-minded, adult company as we navigated the ups and downs of single parenting together.

Unlike me, however, my roommate *was* eager to remarry.

It was the early 2000s, and Internet dating sites were becoming more and more popular. My roommate joined a couple of these sites, paid the necessary membership fees, and began using her profile to connect with fellas online.

I watched her, skeptically, from a distance and noticed that checking these sites became the highlight of her day.

After a while, she began encouraging me to sign up.

I resisted.

We went back and forth for weeks—she would urge and I would politely decline—until finally she pointed out that one of the sites was offering a FREE 2-week trial membership. I acquiesced. I figured 2 weeks was time enough to appease her and *free* definitely appeased me!

I created the most basic of profiles. No frills, fluff, or beauty-queen photo. I uploaded a picture of myself with no makeup, wearing everyday clothes, and with hair that wasn't fixed. The words I chose to describe myself, my hobbies, and the rest of my life were as minimal as they could be.

Once I had my simplistic profile complete, I hit the Publish button and walked away from the computer.

My 14-day countdown began.

Four days in, I noticed I had a message. It was from "Anthony," who lived three states away. We struck up an easygoing dialogue that continued until my free trial expired. By that point, we had exchanged phone numbers.

Anthony was easy to talk to, and despite the fact that I had avoided dating for the past decade of my life, I found that there was a part of me that dreamed of meeting him face to face. I loved talking to him. He made me feel comfortable and safe.

Then, I got cold feet. My first marriage had ended in divorce. I had successfully been navigating life on my own for years, and my children and I were so happy together. Did I really want to risk all that by bringing someone new into our lives?

I emailed Anthony and told him I wasn't interested in talking anymore. Cold turkey. Just like that. As I hit Send on the goodbye email to Anthony, I couldn't help but be a little sad. In our handful of phone conversations, we had just clicked. But I closed the door on those feelings and went on with my life.

I am certain he was absolutely confused and left with whiplash. But then . . .

Six months after being dumped, Anthony popped back up in my email. *Hi there,* he wrote. *I've been thinking about you a lot recently and praying for you. I hope you're doing well. I'd love to be able to chat again sometime soon.*

I was appalled. *Who does this?* I thought my polite "please go away" note from half a year ago was clear, but apparently not. Nothing had changed for me, though. I was resolute in the decision I'd made 6 months before. I responded again with the kindest "please go away . . . I really mean it" that I could muster.

> Do not fear, for I am with you; do not be afraid, for I am your God. I will strengthen you; I will help you; I will hold on to you with my righteous right hand.
> —Isaiah 41:10 (CSB)

Six months passed. Again.

And one day, I opened my inbox to find *another* email from Anthony!

I was flabbergasted! I walked away from my computer, dumbfounded, to ponder this quandary and heard God whisper to me, *You really didn't give him a chance before. Don't worry, I'll be with you and will help you.*

My thoughts were swirling and my heart was pounding as I sat back down in front of the computer screen and typed out the words, *I would love to chat on the phone. Would you like to give me a call?*

And call Anthony did.

That call would kick off a whirlwind, 2-month, long-distance courtship. The feelings that I'd locked behind the door in my heart came rushing out. I couldn't deny how much I liked him.

For the next 8 weeks, Anthony would work his Monday to Friday job and come home every evening to take care of his two little children, for whom he was the sole caregiver. As soon as he clocked out on Friday, he would jump in his car and drive the 7-hour, 460-mile trip to where I was living. He'd check into a hotel and spend the weekend doing things with me, my children, and my church family. He would bid us goodbye late Sunday evening and make the arduous drive back home to grab a few hours of sleep before starting his workweek all over again. This 2-month, physically exhausting marathon was a sacrifice of love, to be sure!

Seven weeks into our long-distance relationship, we both knew we absolutely wanted to spend the rest of our lives together. My diamond engagement ring was nestled gently within the center of the two dozen pink rosebuds that Anthony handed to me as he proposed one beautiful August afternoon.

Two weeks after that, we were married in a small chapel ceremony with a few close family and friends present.

Anthony and I have been married for nearly 20 years now. To this day, I marvel at how God used a two-week window to arrange an online meeting that forever changed my life.

**A time
to love, and
a time to hate**

THE PERFECT DELAY

— By Marcia Gunnett Woodard —

THIS WAS THE answer to my prayer?

A broken-down car that left me stranded in an all-night diner somewhere in the countryside of Indiana? How had I wound up here?

The previous year, I had been in a serious relationship that ended badly. As my heart began to heal, I realized that the man in that relationship wasn't who I truly cared for. I had fallen in love with my best friend, Lloyd.

Lloyd had expressed his feelings for me long before, but I had him firmly ensconced in the "friend zone." Now that I had realized my true feelings, I could see only two things hindering a closer relationship with Lloyd. First, I lived in Chicago, and he lived several hours away, in a little Indiana town not far from the university where we had first met. Second, and most important, I wasn't sure what God thought about the matter.

In my previous relationship, I had rushed ahead of God, forging my own path, ignoring the warning signs that I was taking the wrong path. My experience had taught me a lesson. This time I would wait for God's leading. I would only share my feelings with Lloyd when, and if, God made it clear it was time.

"God, I want to do Your will in Your time. If it's okay for me to tell Lloyd how I feel, have him be romantically unattached when I talk to him," I prayed.

Then I rented a car, took Friday off work, and headed out for Indiana—on Valentine's weekend! I wanted to be certain that I got God's message loud and clear.

The message certainly seemed loud enough now, as I sat in my worthless car. I had only stopped for a cup of coffee, and here I was stuck in the middle of Nowheresville, Indiana, in a rental car that wouldn't start. I called the rental company's assistance number. No one answered. And then it started to snow!

It seemed obvious—if I couldn't even get to my destination, then the answer was no. But I still looked at the situation the way I had planned it on my timeline. God was working the whole thing out in His time. I spent the night in a tiny hotel, in a room wallpapered with pink roses.

The next morning, I woke up to a beautiful, snow-covered world and a rental car that started as soon as I turned the key in the ignition. I was on the road again! Maybe the answer wasn't no!

But the snow was as treacherous as it was beautiful. Twice, I hit a drift on the road and slid into a ditch. Both times, I was able to rock the car out of the drift, with God's help, and a bit of information I remembered from a public service announcement on television.

Eventually, I arrived in the little university town where Lloyd lived. I'd made it! I was still going to be able to spend time with Lloyd and my other friends from the university. But it was 24 hours later than I had planned. Valentine's Day was over, and so, it seemed, was any chance for romance.

I drove by Lloyd's house. He wasn't there, so I found our mutual friend, Sandra, at her work. When I asked if she knew Lloyd's whereabouts, she excitedly told me that he was dating her roommate, Jenna. She launched into a recital of all his romantic gestures: flowers, cards, even an ad in the newspaper.

She finished with, "And they're at the Valentine dinner right now!"

It really seemed the answer to my prayer was no. I said good night to Sandra, leaving the phone number and address of the friend I was staying with to give to Lloyd when he brought Jenna home. He was still my friend, after all, and I still wanted to be able to talk with him like old times.

> If now I have found favor in your eyes, give me a sign that it is really you talking to me.
> —Judges 6:17 (NIV)

The next morning, Lloyd called, wanting to know if I would meet him for lunch. Of course I said, "Yes!"

We met at one of our favorite restaurants. As we settled into our seats, I asked, "So, how are things going?" I expected to hear the same happy story I'd heard from Sandra the night before.

To my surprise his bright smile transformed into a heavy scowl, and he snapped, "Terrible!"

I'm sure my mouth hung open for a moment before I asked, "What's wrong?"

Lloyd began to tell me the story I'd heard—the card, the flowers, the dinner. But his version had a different ending.

"Then, after dinner, when I was taking her home, she announced: 'God told me I have to break up with you, and He said I have to do it tonight.' Can you believe she expected me to fall for that?"

He looked so sad, angry, and confused, but I couldn't help myself. I felt happiness bubbling inside me, and I started to laugh. I laughed at the realization that God had given me His blessing to tell Lloyd how I felt. And I laughed for the joy of a good God, who had made His approval so loud and clear . . . and so unforgettable!

Lloyd wasn't laughing, though. He scowled at me and asked, "What's so funny?"

I quickly told Lloyd of my feelings and explained the prayer I had prayed. By the time I finished my story, he was laughing too. After all, he had been feeling the same way about me for quite some time! Then, oblivious to the rest of the world, we talked and laughed our way through lunch and reached the decision to "see where this thing went."

In mid-March, we decided that we weren't interested in seeing anyone else. On April 12, Lloyd proposed, and in October of that same year, I married the man who had been my friend for 4 years.

Now, more than 40 years later, I'm still so glad that I let God work out His plan in His time.

WE CHOOSE TO LIVE

— By Cristina Moore —

MY HEART RACED as I read the email. It just wasn't possible. How could this happen again? I knew neither my husband nor I were supposed to receive this email; it had been sent to me by mistake. But now that I'd read it, I couldn't take my eyes away. My husband's unit had been selected for a quick-turn mobilization to a combat zone. The email stated they would not have the normal 1-year deployment notification, but that it would be less than 6 months.

I tried to hold back my tears, to swallow my fear, as I sat in the hotel room we were sharing with my two stepchildren and nephew while on vacation in Mexico. My emotions felt so out of place. How could we be sitting in paradise and get this news? How could we be in a place of such joy and peace only to be notified that my husband, Rob, would be heading off to war—again? This would be his third year-long deployment since 9/11. Why did our lives continue to be turned upside down? I looked over to my husband and told him we should go for a walk.

The timing of the email seemed even more tragic because we had scheduled this vacation to get away, to relax before we moved forward with our last attempt to get pregnant. Rob and I had suffered through a miscarriage and several years of infertility before we finally, through God's grace, found a way to seek fertility options.

> You need to persevere so that when you have done the will of God, you will receive what he has promised.
> —Hebrews 10:36 (NIV)

Our journey to this point had been a tumultuous one. In 2004—less than one year after Rob had returned home from a previous deployment—we received notification that the National Guard unit we were both serving in was now slated to deploy to Iraq. Like many others, we had to shut down our home, step away from our civilian jobs, and put our lives on hold. Unlike others, we were a married couple deploying together, making it impossible to consider having a child.

After we returned from our 1-year joint deployment to Iraq, he received a job offer at a large corporation that provided medical insurance benefits that covered fertility treatments. It was an option we had never been able to afford on our own. By this time, it had been more than 3 years since our miscarriage with no sign of pregnancy. Simply put, it was an answer to prayers.

After multiple tests, we started our fertility treatment, and suffered through three painful failed attempts. That should have been the end of the road for us—the fertility clinic had never made four attempts to get the same couple pregnant. But we were blessed to find a doctor that didn't see us as a number—unlike many others struggling through fertility—instead taking the time to get to know us as a couple. He understood the multiple deployments, the heart-wrenching loss with our miscarriage, and the hardships we had suffered through recent years. He fought for the fertility clinic to give us one more chance. This chance—our last chance—was supposed to happen when we came home from Mexico. This could potentially be the final resolution, the prayerful win, to our 7-year battle to get pregnant.

Rob and I sat in the lobby as the tears I could no longer hold back cascaded down my cheeks. How could we think of moving forward? What if he never came home? How could I raise a baby on my own? I felt my heart race in my chest as a whirlwind of emotions and questions crashed over me all at once. I lifted my eyes to Rob as he reached for my hand. He said simply and with conviction, "We choose to live. This war, this deployment, is not going to stop us from moving forward to start a family. We have waited long enough. It is in God's hands." In that moment, I felt peace. A peace and comfort I had not felt in the past 7 years of multiple deployments and failed attempts to get pregnant. I felt, for the first time in my life, that God had this, He had me.

We came home from Mexico and proceeded with our final attempt as Rob prepared for his departure. By this time, we knew he was headed to Afghanistan. He would not be home to give me the required shots after the treatment. He would not be home to deal with the hormonal roller coaster the medications would create. He would not be home to hold my hand when we heard the news if it worked or failed. If we had succeeded, he likely would not be home to see the birth of our child.

By this time, Rob and I were in separate worlds. He focused on preparing himself and his unit for combat, while I went through the motions of everyday life. I remember the day the call came with our test results. I stood alone in a lobby of a public building, holding the phone tightly to my ear, waiting to hear if we were pregnant. The test came back positive. I sat in complete silence as tears of joy ran down my cheeks with the phone to my ear after it had disconnected. My surroundings seemed to disappear. After 7 years, four fertility attempts, and four deployments, we were pregnant. Since Rob was still stateside, I called him immediately to share the news. We were both overjoyed. Little did we know the difficult days we had in front of us.

Rob's deployment would take him to Afghanistan to conduct combat engineering operations. This would require him to lead a team as the operations officer in charge of all counter improvised explosive devices missions to make sure all the routes were clear for

Children are a heritage from the Lord, offspring a reward from him.

—Psalm 127:3 (NIV)

~

our military forces. I would be at home, continuing to serve in the National Guard and focused on having a healthy pregnancy. As part of my military duty, I traveled to a conference where I ended up in the hospital due to complications from my pregnancy. I was convinced I had miscarried again and all our hopes of having a child were lost. I felt numb,

resigned to the fact that this journey had ended. The doctor cleared me to travel home where I could follow up with my doctor.

When I sat in his office the day after I returned home, I was sure I had failed. I knew we had lost this battle. I knew I had lost our baby. After 4 years coming in and out of this office, the room was familiar but cold. I was comforted by the friendly faces of the doctor-and-nurse team that had traveled along this journey with us. As she saw the results on the ultrasound monitor, the nurse held my hand and started to cry. "It's okay. It'll all be okay," I told her as I tried to reach to the depths of my core to find the strength to make it through the news.

I held my breath as the doctor turned the monitor so I could see. At first, I couldn't believe what I was seeing. We had not one, but two healthy babies. The nurse's tears had been tears of joy, not loss. *We're okay. We're having twins.* I don't know how long I had been holding my breath, but the air rushed out of my lungs in relief. There was not a dry eye in the room. This medical team had endured so much right alongside Rob and me. We were able to call Rob so he could hear their heartbeats in real time along with me.

Rob was able to get leave to make it home in time for the birth of our girls and then quickly returned to Afghanistan for another 5 months. We were both forever changed. He knew if he did not make it back home safely, he would miss all those moments with those precious girls, with our miracles. It's not that we didn't always know there was a risk of losing him in combat, it was just something we buried deep. With the girls, it was in the forefront of both our minds for those final days and months of his deployment. At the time, we didn't know it would be his last combat tour. Soon after he came back to us, he retired from the military.

Our story is a little different than most. Our time for war and our time for peace happened at the same time: Rob fighting a war on one side of the world, while I knew the peace of finally achieving our dream on the other. Rob and I both felt God's presence keeping him safe in Afghanistan as he and his soldiers prayed before every mission, just as I felt God at home watching over the health and safety of me and our girls. I'm reminded of what Rob said in that hotel lobby in Mexico: Everything was in God's hands, and, more important, in God's perfect time.

A time for
war, and a
time for peace

RESTITCHED

— By Virginia Ruth —

"I WILL ONLY speak to you with the social worker present." My sister, Lynn, spat out the words, the saliva hitting my face as she stormed out of the hospice family waiting room.

I was in shock. How had our relationship become so strained? It used to be that we could discuss anything. We were similar in so many ways: life philosophies, love of God, even our looks. We understood each other so well that we hardly ever had to explain ourselves to each other. We were cut from the same cloth.

Our relationship had started to unravel while we were tending to our father during his last few weeks on earth. A month earlier, we had both been with Dad in the hospital when it was determined that the pneumonia he suffered was caused by his inability to protect his airway, another manifestation of his Alzheimer's disease. If he ate anything, he would choke. A feeding tube was not an option. He let us know that he wanted to die with dignity, and he chose to go to hospice.

Dad had been in hospice for a couple of weeks when Lynn and I had our altercation. Our conversation had begun innocently enough, with Lynn and I discussing the schedule for Dad's care. But I could tell by the set of Lynn's mouth and her curt tone of voice that she was becoming more irritated. She wanted to discuss alternative treatments for Dad. She wanted physical therapy evaluations and explanations for the rationale behind his treatment from medical doctors. She demanded that Dad not be left alone. Underlying everything she said was the assumption that Dad would be getting better. I was perplexed. We were both nurses. I thought she knew as well as I did that the purpose of hospice was to ease his transition to heaven, not to offer medical treatment. But when I tried to talk to her realistically about what was happening, she lost her temper and stormed out.

Our mother had died suddenly a year and a half earlier. With her death, most of the burden of Dad's care fell to me. While my sister lived 2 hours away, she came to help when she could. When he first became ill, she had been emotionally supportive and joined in decisions regarding the next steps for Dad's care.

When Dad needed to go to assisted living, Lynn had been on board, helping me reaffirm and validate with Dad the need to move. When it was time for Dad to stop driving, she had been my ally as the two of us became the perceived enemies to his independence.

But now that we were facing Dad's death, she was arguing with me at every turn. Her demand for a third-party witness had been building from the day Dad was moved to hospice.

"Why does he need oxygen if he can't have any other treatments?" she asked during the move in. Every time she visited, she rearranged the room, harrumphing at whatever the hospice had provided.

Over and over, she hounded me with questions to ask the medical personnel. She argued with the caregivers at hospice. The few times she visited, she stayed overnight, camping out in the room. When I planned to bring meals over while she visited, she refused to eat with me, and now she was refusing to even speak to me without a third party. After that argument, there was so much tension between us that I couldn't be near her while she was at hospice.

> Bear with each other and forgive one another if any of you has a grievance against someone. Forgive as the Lord forgave you.
> —Colossians 3:13 (NIV)

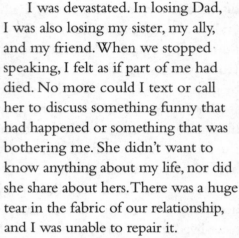

I was devastated. In losing Dad, I was also losing my sister, my ally, and my friend. When we stopped speaking, I felt as if part of me had died. No more could I text or call her to discuss something funny that had happened or something that was bothering me. She didn't want to know anything about my life, nor did she share about hers. There was a huge tear in the fabric of our relationship, and I was unable to repair it.

The only thing that brought us together, even briefly, was church. Nothing pleased our dad more than having "his girls" together in the pew, and we went to our respective churches all our lives. So the Sunday before Dad died, when Lynn had spent the night at the hospice, I asked her to join me at our church. Lynn came and was cordial.

"First be reconciled to your brother," said the pastor as he prepared the communion elements.

Lynn and I looked at each other with tears in our eyes and hugged each other in the pew.

"I am sorry," she whispered in my ear.

"Me too," I said.

The old childhood patterns and discipline of singing and worshiping brought to light what we knew deep in our hearts: our earthly dad and our heavenly Father would want us to be reconciled. Our family bonds went beyond our current frustrations with each other.

Unfortunately, the reconciliation only lasted as long as the service. On Monday, Lynn was back to not speaking to me. For the remainder of the time Dad was in hospice and through his memorial service, Lynn wouldn't confer with me. No stories over the phone or remembrances as we did with Mom's death.

Months later, I was reading Peter's words during my morning Bible time: "Finally, all of you, have unity of mind, sympathy, brotherly love, a tender heart, and a humble mind" (1 Peter 3:8, ESV). I was troubled. How could I have brotherly (or sisterly) love and not be reconciled with my sister?

"Lord, what can I do to repair what seems so torn?" I prayed. The answer came to mind as God gently spoke to my heart: lay aside any bruised feelings, misplaced pride, and righteous indignation. He reminded me that there is always another side to the story and that my relationship with Lynn is far more important than any arguments or having to "be right."

I asked Lynn to meet for lunch. She agreed. We hadn't seen each other in about 5 months, the longest we had ever gone without talking.

After an awkward beginning of inquiries about our families, Lynn broached the subject. "Mom and Dad chose to move closer to you because you and John [my husband] are so stable. You spent time with them. I wish I had, but it seemed they would always be around."

It was the start of a great conversation. She told me about the intense stress she'd been under in her work and home life, situations that had prevented her from visiting Mom and Dad while Mom was alive and from being more present when Dad went into hospice. Meanwhile, I had struggled to keep up with work and home duties while taking care of Mom and Dad. I had been frustrated with her for not being there, and by the time Dad went into hospice I was convinced I was the only one who could care for him. I'd fallen into a resentment loop: the more she couldn't help, the more I became determined to be the solo caregiver, and the more I resented her lack of help. I had shut her out.

By the end of that conversation, we both better understood what the other had gone through, but it would be many years before we fully patched things up. We had to let some time elapse before we could start to see clearly our own roles in our torn relationship. Even now, while we have met many times since that first reconciliation, we are a little cautious in our discussions. There are certain topics, like that hospice altercation, that we have never mentioned. If there are any areas that we think could potentially spark an argument, Lynn or I will preface the conversation with, "I know you may not agree with this . . . "

Painful as the whole process was, I now realize that it was only through God's timing and His lessons of grace and forgiveness that we were able to come together. While I never expected our relationship to fray, the tear allowed God to restitch a stronger bond. The new threads that bind us are more resilient: some are loose in order to handle the pull of disagreements, some contain the stretchiness of grace, and some are taut with the self-control to be kind with our words.

THE POWER OF WEAKNESS

— By Kimberly Shumate —

I WAS EAGER for my trip to Los Angeles to spend precious girl time with my good friend Annalisa. It had been 1 year since I moved away to Oregon, and I missed all my old friends, but especially Anna. We were there for each other through the best and the worst of times—as close as sisters. Now, living in a different state, I had started all over without her. It was a season of reinvention.

After the death of my mother when I was 17, I dropped out of high school and moved around the country searching for a soft place to land. From Eugene, I lived in Atlanta, Seattle, then LA. After my third abortion, I ended up in a midnight clinic in the dregs of Hollywood, hemorrhaging. My life was a mess. It was enough to send me searching for something more than a new address or one more codependent relationship.

Anna was also there when stability finally came—in the form of a Savior who would never leave me, a God who would always love me unconditionally.

Still, 29 years of trauma was buried deep within me. That was evident when, before leaving L.A., out of the blue a panic attack hit me while I was enjoying a rock band at a popular music club. I ended up in the parking lot, sitting on the pavement, unable to move. It was a feeling I had never experienced before.

A girlfriend got me home, but the debilitating anxiety lasted for a few days. I hoped it would never happen again.

After moving back to Eugene, a long-standing eating disorder forced me to seek medical and psychological attention. The hours of counseling that dredged up past mistakes and unmentionable abuse sparked an unnerving vibration that rippled through me. The more I talked about the disturbing events of my life, the worse the symptoms seemed to get.

Isn't everything supposed to get easier with God?

Now, as the calendar brought my LA vacation closer, that familiar, awful feeling was interrupting the excitement. Like static electricity, it buzzed beneath the surface as I tried, in vain, to ignore it. The morning of my flight, I awoke and couldn't move. It was happening all over again, just as it had in that parking lot years ago. Crippled with anxiety, I pulled the covers tightly around me—a blanket of false security that I hoped would comfort me. It didn't.

With thousands of miles under my belt, flying was something I enjoyed—I regularly flew domestically and had twice gone abroad. But this day, with my bags packed and plane ticket paid for, I couldn't get out of bed. I was trapped. I called Annalisa and tried to explain why I wasn't coming, but there was no good explanation. How could I admit that all the bad decisions and regrettable actions from so long ago had left me unable to leave my apartment? The disappointment and confusion in her voice only made matters worse. The conversation was so humiliating that we hung up after a tense exchange. The anxiety attack passed after our phone call ended, as if the decision not to leave gave me permission to relax, take a breath, and know that there was no longer an immediate demand for my strength.

In the coming weeks and months, I could sense two sides at war within me—my troubled past at one end, my faith and future at the other. Which one would win? How long would it take to find out? What would be left of me when it was over?

Curled up on a psychologist's couch, I confided through tears that not only could I *not* get on a plane, I could no longer drive to work (a publishing company I loved) without panic setting in. Going out anywhere was nearly impossible. No more movies at the theater with friends or coffee dates at my favorite café. No more shopping at the mall or dinner at someone's house. I could scarcely go out to buy food at the grocery store a few blocks away. Life had become unbearable.

> When you pass through the waters, I will be with you. . . . When you walk through the fire, you will not be burned.
> —Isaiah 43:2 (NIV)

The worst part was that I couldn't tell anyone what was happening. It's difficult to explain something that you can't rationalize in your own mind. Many times, my friend and coworker Jenn would ask me out for a Saturday morning breakfast or dinner during the week. My answer was always the same: "I can't this week, but definitely some other time." When really, I meant, *I can't imagine doing that anytime soon. I'm too afraid to get in my car and drive to your house. I have terrible anxiety being out in the world. I feel like I'm going to cry if I have to step 1 inch out of my shrinking comfort zone.* I knew it wasn't normal to be afraid of doing things I'd done my whole life, but that didn't change my situation.

I was confined to a prison no bigger than my body—a locked cell with a misplaced key. I rattled the cage and cried inside while friends and coworkers around me went about their business, unaware. I felt like the Academy's greatest actress. And maybe a little flaky, since sometimes I might agree to a gathering, but then cancel at the last minute. My therapist gave me a workbook to help me push past the anxiety, but it was like rowing a canoe across the Pacific Ocean. So much energy to get a mile or two, then an overpowering wave—a spontaneous invitation followed by my failure to commit—would set me reeling backward.

Despair whispered to my heart. My dad had been diagnosed with heart failure. Before long, he would go to join my mom and brother. Who would be left? A God I couldn't see. A Spirit I could barely hear. A Savior I couldn't touch. The light was fading.

As a growing believer, I didn't understand why God would allow things to be so hard. How could He expect me to find a path forward if my only compass was crafted of defective flesh and blood? Surely God knew what I was capable of and, more important, what I wasn't. I went to church, served faithfully in ministry, and was surrounded by spirit-filled Christians. But my personal world remained small and constricted. As it turned out, to win back my freedom would take a lot more than wilting human strength—and a lot less.

After months of suffering, the light bulb went on. I realized that any power I had would always be inadequate, wrapped in instability and insecurities. But it is in that tarnished state that God reveals what we *can* be—courageous and resilient, if only in Him. All I had to do was recognize it, accept it, and possess it. My strength would never be enough if I continued to rely solely upon myself. I had to learn to rely on Him.

In order to break through, I had to learn to stand still. To let go. To wait. And in the irony of quiet submission, my emancipation would come. To release myself to God completely required that I admit my weakness, embrace my limitations, and expect Him to fill in the rest.

In prayer and in my daily routine, I repeated God's truths: "What has happened is my doing" (1 Kings 12:24, NLT). "Do not be afraid or discouraged . . . For the battle is not yours, but God's" (2 Chronicles 20:15, NIV). "Be still, and know that I am God" (Psalm 46:10, NIV). I also committed to memory Psalm 91 in its entirety and spoke it, out loud and often. These promises soothed and fortified me as I battled my way back to a life worth living. When I was on my knees praying for God to lift me up, He would whisper, "I AM." Now I know that going to another level means bowing lower, going deeper, committing to God's will, His way, in His time.

But those who suffer he delivers in their suffering; he speaks to them in their affliction.
–Job 36:15 (NIV)

And just as the spring sun warms the cold winter soil in a gentle thaw, so the tender hand of God began to release me from a season of incarceration.

Pushing against the fear, I resisted the attack that captured so much of what I held dear. My defenses grew and continued to gain ground every time God asked the question, "Do you trust Me?" and I answered, "I do." Slowly, I reclaimed territory stolen from me: Another street. Another place. Another person. . . . Every victory, a celebration. Each defeat, a new opportunity to *let go and let God.*

In the weeks, months, and years that have followed, I've continued to surrender myself daily to the God who knows that I'm only dust. I find freedom in my frailty. I embrace my flaws to magnify God's perfection. I dismiss my own ambition to fulfill His calling. In my many limitations I acknowledge the countless ways that Christ completes what He began. In my darkest nights, His mercy shines the brightest.

One year later, after much prayer, practice, and patience, I boarded a flight bound for California. I had an incredible visit with Annalisa—and got to meet her new baby girl. God's timing was perfect! Anna and I shopped the colorful streets of the fashion district; we ate at funky restaurants filled with eclectic locals; and we reveled in fits of laughter, as if time had forgotten the 2 painful years that had separated us.

Though my inner steel remained warm to the touch from the forging fire of this trial, the process made it plain to me that "with God all things are possible" (Matthew 19:26, NIV).

More than a friendship restored, what I continue to celebrate daily is deliverance with gratitude for the lesson learned: There is a time for war within yourself and a time for peace, and each validates our need for both.

A time for
war, and a time
for peace

THE PECOS ENCOUNTER

— By Emily Tipton Williams —

WHEN I SIGNED up to attend a Christian retreat at the Pecos
Retreat Center in northern New Mexico, I anticipated the opportunity
to be fed and nourished by the Spirit and by the beauty of the red-hued
Sangre de Cristo Mountains, whose name means "Blood of Christ."

I didn't anticipate facing the ire of a red-haired woman!

I had arrived at the retreat a day early and settled into my room.
Later, I wandered down to the Pecos River. I sat on the bank and
watched the overhanging branches dance in the water, relishing the
peacefulness.

However, that peace dissipated the moment I returned to my
room. I discovered I had a roommate.

"I've never been so upset in all my life!" complained the petite
woman with flaming red hair. Her dramatic voice boomed. "I've
come all the way from New York City—been up since 4:00 a.m.—
and you've got your things all over this room. How dare you!"

"I'm sorry," I said, "but the clerk who checked me in said I
wouldn't have a roommate."

"Humph!"

I moved my bags, removed my toiletries from the bathroom,
cleared the top two drawers of the dresser, and stuffed everything
else in an unobtrusive corner.

"I really am quite sorry."

No reply.

I wanted to lash out at her but knew it would do no good. We went to bed in silence.

The next morning, I rose before dawn, dressed, and stayed out of the room. After breakfast I went to the front desk and asked, "Any chance I could change rooms? I prefer a single room. I'd be glad to pay more."

"Sorry, dear, we're full. Are things not working out for you and your roommate?"

"Oh no, everything's just fine."

This unexpected change of events, this woman who had entered my life with no invitation, had diverted my attention from the retreat. Perhaps after a good night's sleep, she would apologize, realizing her rudeness the night before.

But she did not.

I discovered her name was Victoria. *Fitting name,* I thought. *She acts like a queen.*

Her artsy clothes stood out among the others at the retreat. Earthen-tone long skirts and loose-fitting tops with scarves draped her small frame. She walked with an air of authority. Victoria's resonant voice demanded attention whenever she spoke.

I made sure I didn't sit at the same table with her at meals during the first day. At break times, I went in an opposite direction.

"You are so lucky to have Victoria as a roommate," said a woman at dinner. "She's such an interesting person. You know, she just closed as a lead in a successful Broadway play."

We spent another night in our room in silence.

The next day I entered a large room for a workshop and was dismayed to find my roommate there also.

As reflective classical music played, we were instructed to take off our shoes and stand in a circle approximately 3 feet apart. About twenty of us followed the simple stretching exercises, a welcome relief for my stiff muscles. Next our leader announced a scripture. After reading the words, she gave us instructions.

> How good and pleasant it is when God's people live together in unity!
> —Psalm 133:1 (NIV)

"You are to act out the words in silence. I will read the first half, and then pause. Those who choose may enter the center of the circle and pose silently in a descriptive way. Then, after reading the second part, others may join them."

She read the first. "Blessed are the poor in spirit."

Several posed in the middle of the circle looking sad.

"For theirs is the kingdom of heaven."

I watched as others walked to the center, posed, and then returned to their places.

"Blessed are those who mourn."

I went to the center, kneeling with head down, covering my eyes.

"For they shall be comforted."

Someone came and put a warm hand on my back. A touching soul, in search of connection.

Afterward as our group filed out, Victoria approached, and stood in front of me. I turned and started to walk away.

"I've behaved quite badly," she said.

I couldn't believe my ears.

"You certainly have!" I retorted.

She stared at me and then a smile crept onto her face.

We laughed and hugged.

After dinner Victoria and I walked behind the stucco buildings, across a field, and toward the river. The trail paralleled the gently flowing Pecos River. The gurgle of the water provided peaceful background music. As we ambled in silence, I felt so comfortable with this woman who had made my life miserable just 24 hours before. Often more is said in silence than in words.

During our free time the next day, Victoria and I decided to visit the Pecos Historic National Park nearby. The site was on a mesa, on a narrow ridge rising from the floor of a shallow valley that was cut by the meandering Pecos River. Towering mountain peaks surrounded the area. Crumbled remains of one of the largest and most powerful Native American communities in the southwest bore witness to an ancient culture.

The descending sun cast a warm ambiance on the ruins. A slight breeze wafted through the piñon pines. As we reached the top of a hill, we looked down on the massive walls of the old mission church, which stood in defiance to the ravages of time. Sunlight streamed through the roofless structure.

I thought of the many souls who had offered prayers in this place of peace.

The retreat ended too soon. I relished my time with Victoria and was so thankful for the chance to meet this special new friend. She would return to New York City, and I would return to Fort Worth, presumably never to see each other again.

But time proved otherwise.

The next year, while I was visiting my daughter in New York City, I called Victoria.

"Of course, darling. We must get together. I'm free today. Just get on the subway and come right down."

I finally picked the right train and arrived at the correct station. Victoria greeted me with a laugh and big smile. We immediately resumed our budding friendship. After climbing the stairs into the sunlight, Victoria steered me down one of the bustling New York City streets.

"I must show you St. Paul's Chapel before we go to lunch," Victoria proposed.

As we approached the entry of the old colonial church, music filtered out. A professional choir, chamber orchestra, and soloist were rehearsing a Bach cantata for a wedding. They seemed to perform just for us. We sat and listened for almost an hour.

After lunch, Victoria invited me to her home. There, I saw another side of her. The eclectic furnishings included antiques, vintage clothing, a baby grand piano, and memorabilia from her past, including a playbill of her most recent production with Lauren Bacall. We relished our day together, and the time flew by too quickly.

Over a year later I returned to New York City and met with Victoria again. We made another visit to St. Paul's Chapel, this time to grieve in remembrance of the terrorist attack of September 11, 2001. The church was surrounded by devastation, yet the crystal chandeliers hung proudly, undamaged.

No music played this time. Only the slow shuffle of feet and an occasional whisper broke the silence. Red eyes greeted mine when I dared to look. Quilts, posters, and banners made by school children and unknown mourners from every corner of our country hung from the balcony. Glass cases held mementos and letters from all over the world. Exhausted firefighters and workers had left scratch marks on the pews as a memorial. Victoria and I, both in tears, prayed in silence.

And this shared experience again deepened our friendship.

That was the last time I saw Victoria. She died not too long afterward. I mourn her passing, but I rejoice in the friendship we shared. What could have been a memory of frustration instead became a spiritual connection that fed and nourished us for years to come.

ACKNOWLEDGMENTS

Every attempt has been made to credit the sources of copyrighted material used in this book. If any such acknowledgment has been inadvertently omitted or miscredited, receipt of such information would be appreciated.

Scripture quotations marked (CSB) are taken from *The Christian Standard Bible*, copyright © 2017 by Holman Bible Publishers. Used by permission.

Scripture quotations marked (ERV) are taken from *The Holy Bible: Easy to Read Version*, copyright © 2006 by Bible League International.

Scripture quotations marked (ESV) are taken from the *Holy Bible, English Standard Version*. Copyright © 2001 by Crossway Bibles, a division of Good News Publishers. Used by permission. All rights reserved.

Scripture quotations marked (ISV) are taken from the *Holy Bible, International Standard Version*. Copyright © 1995–2014 by ISV Foundation. All rights reserved internationally. Used by permission of Davidson Press, LLC.

Scripture quotations marked (JPS) are taken from *Tanakh: A New Translation of the Holy Scriptures according to the Traditional Hebrew Text*. Copyright © 1985 by the Jewish Publication Society. All rights reserved.

Scripture quotations marked (KJV) are taken from the *King James Version of the Bible*.

Scripture quotations marked (NABRE) are taken from the *New American Bible*, revised edition, © 2010, 1991, 1986, 1970 Confraternity of Christian Doctrine, Inc., Washington, DC. All Rights Reserved.

Scripture quotations marked (NASB) are taken from the *New American Standard Bible®*, Copyright © 1960, 1971, 1977, 1995, 2020 by The Lockman Foundation. All rights reserved.

Scripture quotations marked (NCV) are taken from *The Holy Bible, New Century Version*. Copyright © 2005 by Thomas Nelson. Used by permission. All rights reserved.

Scripture quotations marked (NIV) are taken from *The Holy Bible, New International Version*. Copyright © 1973, 1978, 1984, 2011 by Biblica, Inc. Used by permission of Zondervan. All rights reserved worldwide. zondervan.com

Scripture quotations marked (NKJV) are taken from *The Holy Bible, New King James Version*. Copyright © 1982 by Thomas Nelson. Used by permission. All rights reserved.

Scripture quotations marked (NLT) are taken from the *Holy Bible, New Living Translation*. Copyright © 1996, 2004, 2007 by Tyndale House Foundation. Used by permission of Tyndale House Publishers Inc., Carol Stream, Illinois. All rights reserved.

Scripture quotations marked (NRSVUE) are taken from the *New Revised Standard Version, Updated Edition*. Copyright © 2021 National Council of Churches of Christ in the United States of America. Used by permission. All rights reserved worldwide.

A NOTE FROM THE EDITORS

We hope you enjoyed *In God's Time,* published by Guideposts. For more than seventy-five years, Guideposts, a nonprofit organization, has been driven by a vision of a world filled with hope. We aspire to be the voice of a trusted friend, a friend who makes you feel more hopeful and connected.

By making a purchase from Guideposts, you join our community in touching millions of lives, inspiring them to believe that all things are possible through faith, hope, and prayer. Your continued support allows us to provide uplifting resources to those in need. Whether through our communities, websites, apps, or publications, we inspire our audiences, bring them together, and comfort, uplift, entertain, and guide them. Visit us at guideposts.org to learn more.

We would love to hear from you. Write us at Guideposts, P.O. Box 5815, Harlan, Iowa 51593 or call us at (800) 932-2145. Did you love *In God's Time*? Leave a review for this product on guideposts.org/shop. Your feedback helps others in our community find relevant products.

Find inspiration, find faith, find Guideposts.

Shop our best sellers and favorites at
guideposts.org/shop
Or scan the QR code to go directly to our Shop